We hear often about the parenting Judy Schumacher knows this period of development is a time of exciting growth and discovery, both for children and parents. *Terrific Toddlers!* shines with insight and overflows with practical tips to help parents promote their children's competence and their own peace of mind. A gift to toddlers and the adults who care for them!

Marti Erickson, PhD
Director Emerita, Irving Harris Programs, University of Minnesota
Co-host of Mom Enough™ (www.momenough.com)

Terrific Toddlers! provides a treasure trove of down-to-earth practical advice for parents as they navigate their way through the invigorating, fun, and mystifying adventures of toddlerhood. It's easy to read expert advice. It's like having a parent coach at your fingertips.

David Walsh, PhD
Psychologist and best-selling author

As described by Selma Fraiberg in her classic book from 1959, these years are truly "The Magic Years." In her new book, *Terrific Toddlers!*, Judy Schumacher has captured this magic as the toddler explores her ever expanding new world, while giving her parents real world approaches to manage the challenges that will certainly arise. By capturing the toddler's temperament variations, developmental tasks and behavioral challenges, Ms. Schumacher has given parents both understanding and direction. A must read for all parents and caregivers entering into this special and unforgettable age.

W. Brooks Donald, MD
Developmental/Behavioral Pediatrics HealthPartners Clinics
Minneapolis, MN

I've read lots of books on toddlers, but *Terrific Toddlers!* is by far the best, because I now understand how my child is *feeling* as she goes through each developmental stage. I also have many more ideas on how to handle different toddler behaviors. I am now a much more patient and empathetic mother.

Maureen Brown Boxrud, Parent St. Paul, MN

TERRIFIC TODDLERS!

SIMPLE SOLUTIONS
PRACTICAL PARENTING

Judy Schumacher, MA

in collaboration with

MARJORIE HOGAN, M.D.
and JUDSON REANEY, M.D.

ISBN: 978-1-4834-7534-9 (sc)
ISBN: 978-1-4834-7533-2 (e)

Library of Congress Control Number: 2017915590

Because of the dynamic nature of the Internet, any web addresses or links contained in
this book may have changed since publication and may no longer be valid. The views
expressed in this work are solely those of the author and do not necessarily reflect the
views of the publisher, and the publisher hereby disclaims any responsibility for them.

This book is a work of non-fiction. Unless otherwise noted, the author and the publisher
make no explicit guarantees as to the accuracy of the information contained in this book
and in some cases, names of people and places have been altered to protect their privacy.

Any people depicted in stock imagery provided by Thinkstock are models,
and such images are being used for illustrative purposes only.
Certain stock imagery © Thinkstock.

Lulu Publishing Services rev. date: 10/25/2017

DEDICATION

Judson Reaney was a wonderful, well-loved, and well-respected behavioral pediatrician, whose warmth, keen sense of humor, and deep and abiding commitment to his young patients and their families has left a positive and indelible mark on the communities he served.

As our partner in writing this book, Jud shared his wisdom and experience as we worked to get the message out to all parents and caregivers about their critical role in the success of their children, especially during one of the most important developmental stages of life, twelve to thirty-six months of age.

Tragically, Jud did not live to see this book published. He died on February 24, 2012, of pancreatic cancer.

We dedicate *Terrific Toddlers!* to Jud. He left a legacy of love for all who knew him.

TABLE OF CONTENTS

ACKNOWLEDGEMENTS

I want to acknowledge my own two terrific toddlers, Erica and Andrew, whom I loved raising and from whom I have learned so much about living with and loving children through all the challenging yet wonderful developmental stages. I would also like to thank my husband, Tony, for being such a wonderful father to our children and for his love and support throughout all the years of our long and loving marriage. Thanks also, to Margie and Jud for their love, friendship, and wise counsel throughout the writing of this book.

Judy Schumacher

I want to thank my friends Judy and Jud, my husband, Dave Griffin, for his warm and wise co- parenting, and my four children and innumerable patients of all ages who taught me everything I know.

Margie Hogan

One of the greatest pleasures of my marriage to Jud was watching his joy in serving children. In Margie and Judy, he found kindred spirits. I know he would want to thank them for giving their precious time to write this book and for living out their love for all children of the world. In the last few years, Jud became very committed to the renewal of those who give their lives unselfishly in work with others. He gained so much knowledge and support from the work of Parker Palmer. Jud, above all, was a family man. He spoke weekly to his parents and sisters and always had time for his daughter, Kat, and myself. I know he would thank his family for their incredible bonds and strong support. We, in turn, would thank him for the deep and unwavering love he gave to all of us.

Susan Reaney

PREFACE

Everyone has a passion or two in life—something that "hooks" you and doesn't let go. My passion is children—particularly toddlers, ages twelve to thirty-six months. Research tells us that the first three years of life are absolutely critical in a child's development. These years create the very foundation upon which each child's life is built. Every touch, every word, every day during this period in a tiny human being's life impacts that child one way or another.

As I studied this stage of child development, and had the privilege of raising two toddlers myself, I realized not just the crucial importance of this time in every person's life, but also the complexity that it brings. It's not easy. Some days are great and some days are devastating. Some days we think we're the most brilliant parents ever born, and other days we feel we've completely failed. Neither, of course, is completely true. I wasn't a perfect parent. No one is perfect . . . at anything.

And I certainly don't have all the answers—no one does. The one thing I do know is that every child deserves the very best we can provide. Toddlers are amazing little creatures. So much is going on in their little minds, hearts, and bodies that it's hard to keep up with them. That's why I wrote this book—because the more parents and caregivers know and the better they understand what their toddler is seeing and hearing, feeling and learning during this stage, the better job they will do as positive, loving guides in their children's lives.

The advice in these pages is meant to inform, not to dictate. You are your child's first and most important teacher. You will decide what is right for your child and your family. Just remember to enjoy the toddler stage—it's a fascinating adventure!

CHAPTER 1

Who IS My Twelve- to Thirty-Six-Month-Old?

Parenting is a privilege and a challenge. From birth forward, parenting is a constant adjustment to a changing child. The toddler stage, in particular, is notorious for rapid, unpredictable, and oh-so-cute transformation.

Your toddler will grow from babyhood into personhood in twenty-four months. You will see your little one change from a usually dependent, cooperative baby to a much more independent, curious, active, and fascinating person. These children are typically eager to learn new things and will want to do everything themselves, rather than let you do it for

> This stage of child development, twelve to thirty-six months, is one of the most exciting, frustrating, amazing, joyful, and challenging ages you and your child will experience.

them. They'll be completely cooperative one minute and surprisingly stubborn the next. You can expect them to grow a great deal physically, and because they see and feel their bodies growing and changing, they feel more grown up and will want to try everything grown-ups do.

Parents also need to keep in mind that parenting is a tough job. You'll make mistakes, but you can learn from each mistake and determine to handle it better the next time. The more you learn about what to expect in each stage of your child's development, and especially *why* certain behaviors happen, the better prepared you will be to deal with changes in your child and in your relationship as you move through the years together.

Parents can sometimes expect too much of their little ones, especially if they don't know what kinds of behaviors and changes to expect at different ages. When children don't behave as parents expect them to, the result can be anger, unnecessary punishment, and sometimes even more unrealistic expectations.

Because the toddler stage of development is so full of

This stressful situation can usually be avoided if parents set aside a little time, even once a year, to read a book or watch a video on what to look for during the *next* year of their child's life. It will be well worth the time for both parent and child.

change for the child and can be challenging at times for parents, it's important to learn about the normal behavior changes to expect during this time period. Several very important ingredients must be included in any good parenting recipe, and these need to be applied consistently, with all children, regardless of particular personality traits.

- An important ingredient for effective parenting is remembering that every child is different.

Every child and every family is different, so it is very important to try different approaches for different challenges.

Children can be very similar in many ways, but even identical twins are not exactly the same. That's why it is so important to try different approaches for each child. You'll find it's worth the effort, because certain things work better with some children than others. Remember that each parent is different as well!

Situations change, families move, jobs change, and each additional child born into the family changes how families interact.

At this point, I would like to clarify what I mean by "family." Families come in all sizes, colors, and shapes: two-parent biological families, single-parent biological families, grandparent-as-parent families, gay and lesbian families, other-relatives-as-parent families, older-siblings-as- parent families, adoptive families of all combinations, and other combinations of people who make up a family.

> **M**y favorite description of a family is from a six-year-old: "A family is a group of people who love each other."

The terms "parent" and "caregiver" are used frequently throughout this book, to refer to the person who is raising the child. Please insert the term that applies to your family as you read this book.

> **U**nconditional love is an essential parenting ingredient.

- One of the most critical parenting ingredients is unconditional love.

This means that, no matter how our children behave, no matter what they accomplish or fail to accomplish, no matter what circumstances we find ourselves in, we, as parents, need to provide love and support for our children. The comment, "If you do that, I won't love you anymore," is a very hurtful statement that chips away at all the love, trust, and security that you and your children have built over the months and years of

> **C**hildren need to know they can make mistakes without losing your love.

your lives. It is absolutely necessary to let kids know that certain behaviors are not acceptable, but always make sure you make it clear that you love the child but not the behavior.

Encouragement and praise, especially when your kids do something well, are also an important part of effective parenting. Telling your children that you're proud of them and that they're doing a good job does wonders for your child's self-confidence.

Be honest, however—don't make something up. "Catch them" being a good friend, saying something nice, using good judgment, or thinking about someone else's feelings. Children enjoy being praised and will continue to look for positive ways to behave in order to get that praise.

> **L**ook for opportunities to compliment your children.

- Taking time to talk with and listen to your children is critical to effective parenting. Toddlers have important things to say, not to mention, sometimes very funny things!

Listening gives you a window into your child's personality, likes and dislikes, and hopes and dreams. Keeping the lines of communication open to any subject helps your children feel free to talk about feelings, problems, or situations that are confusing or complicated. You want them to feel comfortable coming to you for information as they get older as well, instead of going to their friends, whose facts may not be accurate.

> **B**y listening to your children from birth onward, you can help to ensure a lifetime of effective communication—one of the most precious gifts you can give your child.

Communication between parent and child is critical, of course, but so is communication with other important people in your child's life. Let's take health care providers, for example. Parents are human and cannot be expected to know exactly what to do or when to do it for everything that comes up regarding their children, especially with medical issues. When you do call your doctor or nurse with a question, if you don't receive a thorough answer, or if you're made to feel like you're bothering them with your question, consider changing doctors or clinics. It's important that you feel comfortable asking questions because you may be able to prevent major health problems by taking action with small problems early. Parents know their children better than anyone else and their intuition is often right on. The best pediatricians and nurses ask critical questions of the parent and listen carefully to the answers.

Health care providers are busy, but if you've tried everything you can think of, or if you are worried about your child's health, please call for help. It is your right and responsibility as a parent to see to your child's needs.

- Setting limits is another crucial ingredient in raising children, who need and want limits but will go out of their way to avoid them.

Children who do not have limits on their behavior and don't pay consequences for misbehaving are often unhappy and insecure because they don't know how far to go in any situation. A child's job is to keep pushing the limits until someone stops him, which often creates a situation where there's considerable anger and crying, and everyone is unhappy. If you consistently set clear limits, you can often prevent this type of situation. Setting limits such as not going near the street, not touching the hot stove, or not playing with matches are obvious safety limits for little ones.

Limits such as when to take a nap, when to use a quiet voice (an "inside" voice) or a loud voice (an "outside" voice), what words or behaviors to use, which foods are for snacks (ice cream!) and which ones are for dinner (ice cream!), or when and if

> Children need and want limits. Set clear limits and apply them consistently.

they're allowed to have a treat at the store are parental decisions, based on the values and lessons parents decide to teach their children. Even though it can be difficult to set and then to enforce limits, it's crucial for parents to be in control. It helps to remember that you are a parent, not your child's best friend. Once the limits are set and maintained, everyone is happier.

- Teaching values like respect, honesty, kindness, and generosity, and above all, to model these values yourself are basic parenting ingredients.

Simply behave like you want your children to behave. Children who grow up without values are at a huge disadvantage. Understanding from a very young age how important it is to treat others

> Children learn best from watching the behavior of those around them—they are the best mimics in the world!

with respect, to share, to be kind and generous, or to comfort someone who is sad or lonely are basic human relationship skills that are needed throughout life. Children who are taught to be kind, compassionate, and generous feel good about themselves, find it easier to make friends, and are often more comfortable in social situations. Bullies generally don't feel very good about themselves and lack self-esteem. Bullying is preventable!

Try to remember that when you must discipline (teach) your kids, do it thoughtfully, while trying to keep your own anger or disappointment under control. There is a range of opinion on using time-outs for young children. Some people don't use them at all and others believe parents should just take a break with the child to calm everyone and then go back to playing. Others use them very effectively. If you do decide to use a time-out, use it sparingly, as just one of the methods you use, not the only method. You can stop the play and put your child in a chair, away from the fun, out of reach of any toys or books. If you put her in her bedroom, make sure she sits on the bed with no toys or playthings within reach. If you choose to use time-outs, be reasonable about how long the time-out lasts. The general recommendation is no more than one minute longer than the age of the child. For example, if your child is three, the maximum time-out should be four minutes. You'd be surprised at how long four minutes can seem to a three-year-old.

The idea with a time-out is to take children away from the fun, so they learn that their fun stops if they misbehave, and that creates a reason for them to behave— so they can continue to play, uninterrupted. After the time-out, make sure to talk calmly with your child about what just happened, so they understand what they did wrong and how to do it better the next time. Each time this happens, use it as a "teachable moment" so that your child can learn the lesson you want her to remember.

> Time-outs for toddlers should be no longer than three to four minutes.

Another good recommendation for parents of toddlers is to pick your battles. What you do not want is a constant stream of fights every day.

> Kids need to win the argument sometimes, when the situation is not dangerous or harmful to them.

You show respect for your children by listening to their explanation and at times, by being persuaded by their arguments. This way, you teach your little ones that everyone wins sometimes and everyone loses sometimes, but that everyone needs to listen to each other and occasionally compromise.

One of the most important points to keep in mind whenever you interact with your children is to use a positive approach. Taking time to sit down with your child on your lap, explaining calmly but firmly that certain behaviors are not acceptable, and then discussing exactly how to better handle a similar situation the next time helps your child feel respected instead of shamed.

Your child can then feel better about herself and everyone stays calmer and more positive. After a few repetitions of this method of teaching (teaching a toddler anything requires lots of repetition, and thus, patience!), the child should eventually learn this approach and begin to use it without parental help.

> **A** positive approach gives children a chance to learn a better way to do things, a chance to change the behavior, and then to be praised for behaving well.

Positive parenting includes rewarding your child for good behavior. Whenever someone compliments you, an adult, on a job well done, it makes you feel good. It even makes you feel like doing your best every time, especially when someone takes the time to tell you how much they appreciate it. Children are the same way. They need to hear you say, "Thanks for behaving so well. I'm really proud of you. Keep trying, you're doing a great job. You figured that out all by yourself—you're so smart!" These important comments make your children feel good about who they are and what they can do for themselves.

Look for the chance to praise your kids for good behavior and they will continue to behave well (not always, of course) to hear more praise from you. The opposite is also true: If you never compliment your children, they have no reason to try their best. They know you'll never praise them for

> **E**xtra hugs and pats on the back also make kids feel good about themselves.

the good job they've done, so why bother? Your children need to know you're on their side, that you'll always be there to encourage them.

Children need encouragement, but just as importantly, they need to *work* at things in order to learn. Let your child struggle a bit; try not to jump right in to help. Struggling for a while in order to succeed is an important lesson. You will actually teach your child to give up easily if you help too soon or too often. Give them the message that you know they can do it, and they'll be much more determined to live up to your expectations. For example, if your child gives up too easily while putting a jigsaw puzzle together, you might say, "Look, Siri, you've put in two pieces all by yourself! I'll bet you can find the next piece and make it three!" Set standards high (but always within their reach) and your children will try to meet them. And after you tell them they can do it—as long as they try, even if they don't succeed—compliment them for trying. If you criticize them when they come up short, when they are really trying, they'll decide they can't do it and you will have actually helped them to fail.

The tried and true tactic of counting to ten or telling yourself to calm down before you react, especially in a stressful situation (and there may be many of those in the toddler years) is an excellent way for parents to think before they act or say something they will later regret. One great technique is to *think about how your child must be feeling at that moment*; it will also help you to be more understanding and more patient with your little ones. Once again, remember what great mimics kids are. The more positive parents can be, the more positive their children will be. Parents, you are constant role models for your children—either positive or negative. The choice is up to you.

> **W**e need to encourage children to try new things and to work at them, and we also need to praise them for trying—*whether they succeed or fail.*

- A good sense of humor is also an essential parenting ingredient!

Toddlers say and do outrageously funny things—enjoy them! It is much more difficult to raise children without a sense of humor. You can frequently bring children out of a bad mood by using humor to distract them. Just like adults, children love to laugh. When you model humor as a coping skill (whenever it's appropriate, of course), your little ones will learn how and when to use it with others. Humor can be a lifesaver in many situations.

Don't miss the joy of parenting because you're worried about doing everything perfectly. Love, trust, respect, and good humor will help get you and your child over the rough spots—and there *will* be some rough spots! Also, try not to judge yourself too harshly. When you have a bad day with your toddler, try to think (later, when you're calmer) about what happened, why it happened, and how you could handle it more effectively the next time.

> **L**augh *with* your toddlers, not at them; but do remember to laugh.

If we look at our overall parenting, instead of dwelling on a bad day, we realize that we usually do a pretty decent job of loving and caring for our kids. Parenting is a roller-coaster ride—exciting, fun, and sometimes scary, but well worth the price of admission!

> **R**emember to forgive and forget and start over with a new, positive attitude every morning.

Now, back to the toddler. Children learn from those around them and will repeat the words they hear and behave the way those around them behave. Toddlers want to try to do everything grown-ups do, but they won't be able to. Sometimes, just letting them try will be enough—sometimes, it won't.

For example, because your child has watched you take time to dress up and look in the mirror before you go out, your child will probably want to look just right, too. Tensions may rise as toddlers change their minds three times about what they want to wear, argue about which dress or shirt goes with which tights or pants, and fuss, whine, or worse yet, stand naked in the middle of the room, flatly refusing to cooperate. At this point, if you begin to lose your patience and demand that they put something on so you can leave, they may very well throw a tantrum—just exactly the thing you need right then.

When your toddler chooses a pink flowered shirt and a fake raccoon cap to go with red-and-green plaid pants, try not to let on that you think you'll be voted the worst fashion parent of the year for letting them out of the house looking like that. Anyone who has gone through the toddler years knows that you *gradually* teach your child how to dress, and besides, a certain amount of experimentation is good for a kid! (By the way, practice makes perfect . . . by the time they reach adolescence, it will probably be "in" to wear nothing that matches.) Furthermore, anyone who would seriously judge your parenting skills on what your child wears is not a real pal anyway!

> **Y**ou can usually avoid this situation by taking time the night before to help your little ones choose exactly what they will be wearing, right down to the color of socks. Lay them out at night to save time in the morning.

One main objective of this book is to help parents choose the struggles that are really important for their child's development and to avoid the rest. The fewer arguments you have to face, the more smoothly your days and nights will go. When children and parents are happy with one another, positive things begin to happen: both are more willing to cooperate, a more loving, trusting, and respectful attitude develops, and your relationship grows closer and stronger.

One important thing to keep in mind as you parent your toddler: remember to take care of *yourself*, too. In order to run this toddler marathon, you need to get enough rest, eat well, exercise to keep your stress level down, and try to take some time for yourself. Friends or family can step in for a short time to give you a break—it's good for everyone.

> **L**ove, trust, and respect are three of the key ingredients to a happy, healthy family unit.

11

CHAPTER 2

Temperament and Uniqueness

Something that makes each child unique is their temperament or personality. Remember, for a moment, the first time you looked through the window of a newborn nursery. As early as a few hours old, these babies are behaving differently from one another. Some are sleeping peacefully, some are wide awake, lying quietly, and some are screaming loudly for attention. It's fascinating to watch all these different little personalities in action.

Babies will sometimes be happy and sometimes sad, sometimes hungry and sometimes not. They will be wide awake when you think they should be tired, and asleep when you expect them to be up and running. Each

> **B**abies are born to be themselves and no one else, with personalities all their own.

day is different and usually unpredictable, just like it is for adults. Both adult and toddler behaviors change depending upon many things—mood, fatigue, hunger, etc. We respond to these things in different ways, dictated by our temperament and personality.

Each child is born with a distinct temperament and personality. For example, there's the "slow to warm up" child, who needs to start slowly in the morning and gradually move toward breakfast and then some activity an hour later. By the time afternoon rolls around, this toddler is often running from one thing to the other, chatting and playing happily.

Then there's the child whose engine is running full throttle before he even gets out of bed in the morning. He begins talking and grabbing toys or books before he is even out of his room and wants everyone else to play while his sleepy parents are still trying to pry open their eyelids. By afternoon, he's crashed into a two-hour nap, while the adults around him take a deep breath and enjoy the quiet.

Another type of personality is a child like Zoe, who is upset by surprises and does not handle change well. A change in her daily schedule, which clothes to wear, or which foods she thought she would be eating that day can cause a tantrum or spoil an afternoon.

Sometimes toddlers who dislike change can come up with their own solution. Although this can be hard to do, it's important to try to prepare a child like Zoe for changes she might have to deal with during the day, so she can think about it ahead of time and not be caught off guard. It will be worth the trouble and help the day go more smoothly.

> Children who are more rigid may need extra preparation for a change in plans.

One of our little friends, Peter, found it hard to switch from one thing to another. For example, he would wear only sweatshirts and sweatpants—they were just more comfortable than other clothes (some adults agree!). One day, before school, he came down to breakfast with a big hole in his sweatpants. When his mom pointed this out, he went back to his room and returned looking rather plump. He had simply put on another pair of sweatpants *over* the pair with the hole in them! That way, he didn't have to change his plan for the day. Instead of his mom telling him to take one pair off, she just let him do what he was comfortable doing—she let him be him—and he went to school wearing two pair of sweatpants and a big smile, as well.

> Some toddlers are especially sensitive to light or sound or even touch.

There are also children who are super-sensitive, and nothing ever seems quite right. They never seem to slip into any routine, they are very light sleepers, and they are easily frustrated.

Jody, for example, could not stand anything around her waist. She refused to wear pants of any kind and wore a dress every day—with only socks, not even tights, which was a challenge to her parents from October through March in Minnesota! They finally bought her snow pants with no waistband so she wouldn't freeze during the winter.

Jody didn't choose to be this way; she was born with a certain temperament that brought with it sensitivity to things that touched her skin. Parents and caregivers need to work with the personality that comes with their child, and not try to change their child into someone they're not. Just as adults come in different sizes, shapes, and personalities, so do kids. Remember not to get frustrated with your little ones for being different or if they are more challenging because of things like the example above. Respect your children for who they are and try to be flexible. People who are persistent and intense as children often turn out to be very competent adults, who are organized and know how to stick with things to get them done.

Each child is born equipped with personality traits that control the way they react to the world around them.

> **U**ntil they have had a few years to learn the rules and regulations of respectful behavior, children can respond only as their given personality dictates.

Remembering this can help you to be more patient when they cry or need lots of attention, because they are not behaving this way to somehow get back at you or deliberately make you angry. They are simply responding to their own basic needs and personality. Again, *thinking about how your child is feeling* can help you to be more patient and understanding.

> **I**n addition, your child will have different needs every day—just like you do. Try your best to provide for those needs.

No two days will be exactly alike. Just as you would like other people to be aware of your needs and meet them every day, try to be aware of the cues your child gives you.

Positive parenting means encouraging kids to be who they really are—not just a copy of *you*. This means letting them try new things, things that interest them, even if they don't interest you. It also means they may not want to do things just like you do. Provide a variety of play experiences and simple toys and watch what happens—your children will show you what *they* are interested in.

Talking and Listening

Praising little ones for talking and helping them to learn new words and phrases can become a fun game for everyone. It's critical to helping your toddler enjoy the process of learning to talk.

Between twelve and thirty-six months of age, one of the most exciting and obvious changes you will see is the development of language. By eighteen months, most children are using single words such as "ball," "go," or "play," and sometimes using several words in a sentence. Combined with facial expressions and hand gestures, these words can communicate a great deal. If you respond by listening carefully to the words being used, repeat the word, and praise your toddler for the effort, your child will learn that talking will get your attention. Because toddlers like and need attention, they will keep experimenting with words in order to get it.

One of the most important things you can do to help your toddlers learn to speak well is to give them your time. It takes time to learn that certain sounds and words mean certain things.

You don't have to be a speech therapist to help your child learn to talk. Simply use everyday situations to teach words and sounds.

15

Parents need to take time to actually teach their toddler how to make sounds and pronounce words.

When parents speak slowly and deliberately, most toddlers will watch their parents' mouths to see where the sound is coming from. Often they will try to make the same sound themselves. Try to use the same method each time you teach a new word, so that it becomes a kind of fun game. Children who have fun while they learn something new, learn better and more quickly than when they are forced to do something they don't enjoy.

Remember that different children begin speaking at different times. Many toddlers will have some single words by their first birthday, like "Mama" or "Dada," and will be putting together short sentences by age two, such as "Go bye-bye car." Speech development varies widely, so don't panic if your toddler isn't speaking as well as the toddler up the street. Warning: comparing your toddler with other children, even their own older siblings, is not helpful. Remember that each child is different and will develop on his or her own schedule.

The most basic ingredient in learning to talk is simply hearing words spoken. Talking to your child, regardless of the topic, especially from birth to age five, helps your child's brain develop. "Parentese," or exaggerated "baby talk," is used when parents deliberately lengthen the vowel sounds when they pronounce a word. For example, you might say, "Baaaatle" for "bottle," "baaaaaby" for baby," or "mooooore" for "more." This helps your little one begin to learn the difference between specific sounds. It helps her brain recognize vowel and consonant combinations. However, this works well only up to about age two, when you will need to make sure you are pronouncing all words correctly so your child learns the correct word pronunciation going forward.

Parents should also label objects for the child: "Look at the moon" or "See the pretty flower." Reading books to your child is a great way to point out different objects and identify them while you read the story. Follow your child's lead—if she points at her stroller, say, "Yes, that's your stroller." If your baby says, "Buh" and reaches for her bottle, you might say, "Baaattle. Do you want your bottle?" Repetition is very important in learning speech. You'll learn that babies and toddlers can understand many words well before they can actually say the word.

Another way to add words to your child's vocabulary is to give the same message different ways. For example, "Emma, please give Daddy the book." "Bring the book to him." "Give it to Daddy." "Thank you, Emma. You gave the book to Daddy."

For younger toddlers, usually before fifteen or sixteen months, it's helpful to move or jiggle an object while saying the word. For example, "Here comes the mouse" while making the toy mouse dance in front of your toddler. This helps your child learn the name of the toy while you play. Remember, a child's play is her work—she's learning while she plays. Make the learning fun and she'll want to learn more!

Decades of research have shown that the more words children hear and know by the time they enter kindergarten, the better prepared they are for success in school and in life. Looking directly into the eyes of your child and talking softly and gently should begin the first time you hold the baby in your arms. From the day of birth, your child learns how to communicate by watching you. Even very young children can sense how important they are to you when you value them enough to give them your undivided attention.

> **W**hen you need to talk seriously with your toddlers, get down to their eye level or bring them up to your eye level and look straight into their eyes so they know that the conversation you're having is important.

Of course, this is not always possible when they're running out the door, jumping on the bed, or scampering from swing to monkey bars at the park. There are quiet times, however, when you can really talk and listen to each other and have a wonderful conversation, just the two of you.

> **O**ne of the best ways to teach words is by reading books to your children.

Pointing out words and pictures and having your toddler repeat the names of

17

animals and other objects is a great way to stimulate brain development and help your little one learn new words. Reading books is a wonderful way for a child to hear thousands of words and begin to understand the connection between letters on a page, words in a sentence, and stories in a book. Reading books *every day* is important to help your child develop a love of books and stories and to develop a larger vocabulary, which is critical in helping them to be ready to learn in school and to become better readers, writers, and spellers as they get older. Reading a book or two to your child, or just telling them a story at bedtime, relaxes your child and is a great way to signal that it's time to quiet down and go to sleep. Keeping books in the car or reading books on the bus is also a great way to distract your children on long trips—or even short ones.

Remember that it feels good to your toddler to have you close, to see your face, and to hear your voice. Because we live in such a busy, fast-paced world, it's very important to deliberately set aside quiet times to really connect with your little ones. Communication is used not only to exchange information, but also to express many emotions, including your love for your child.

There is also another highly recommended method to teach your babies and toddlers to communicate before they can begin to use words. It's Baby Sign Language, based upon the American Sign Language (ASL) method of communication. Babies need to communicate with us from birth onward to get their needs met, but most babies don't begin to use words until around twelve months or later. When babies try to tell you what they need or want but don't have the words to do it, they can become very frustrated, which can often result in crying or tantrums. Teaching your child sign language provides a wonderful way to tell you what they need without words, reducing frustration for both parent and child. You say the word as you sign it, so it doesn't slow down language development; it simply provides an additional way to communicate that word. Studies show that signing strengthens speech development connections in the brain, builds confidence, and encourages social development as babies learn to communicate with parents and then each other.

There are many books, videos, and websites available that teach

Baby Sign Language, which is now being used by more and more people, because it's easy to learn for both parent and child and it works so well. Just remember that you need to make it fun and be consistent, using the word and the sign at the same time, every time, to reinforce learning. Again, all children are different and learn at their own pace, but using sign language is an effective way to reduce frustration and strengthen parent and child bonding.

Today, with the increasing diversity in our communities and all over the world, many families speak more than one language in their homes. Research shows that toddlers and young children have the ability to learn more than one language at a time. Learning words in any language stimulates brain development. In fact, it's easier to learn multiple languages when a child is very young. In some childcare centers in very diverse communities, toddlers who have teachers who speak different languages are able to move from one teacher to another and speak to each in their own language! It's a great gift to your child to learn more than one language at an early age.

Teaching (Discipline)

The topic of discipline is a controversial one. Discipline means many different things to different people. To some, unfortunately, the word means to spank or to hit a child. To others, it brings images of the military, of strict obedience and control. In the family, its meaning should be very simple.

The reason discipline is described as teaching is because every time your children do something you *don't* want them to do, you need to take the time

> **D**iscipline means "to teach."

to teach them what you *do* want them to do. This is how children learn from their mistakes. It also helps them understand why you want them to behave a certain way and helps them avoid making the same mistake in the future.

If your goal is to teach instead of to punish, then the approach will be calmer and the child will learn two important things: how a loving person handles a conflict positively, and how and why not to do it again.

If the goal is to punish instead of to teach, then sometimes anger takes over. It is often difficult to stay calm when your child misbehaves, but it's so important if you want your little one to learn from the incident.

When they are spanked, children learn that hitting is the way to solve problems.

If there were a better alternative than hitting your children to teach them proper behavior, wouldn't you want to use it? All parents love their children and want the best for them. If you want to teach your toddler, you do have to stay in control if that child is to learn. But this doesn't mean that you can never show frustration or anger toward your child, or that your child can never express the same toward you. You need to teach the appropriate way to express those

The right words, used firmly and carefully, teach our children the lessons we want them to remember. Hitting children teaches them that it's okay to hit others.

feelings by showing that you, as the role model, can state those feelings calmly, without losing control. Your little ones need to know when they make mistakes, but that's just the point—you tell them firmly that what they have done is wrong, and then you tell or show them how they should have acted.

We're back to the importance of role modeling—if a child learns to hit from watching the parent hit, then hitting becomes the way that same child will now settle arguments with friends or brothers and sisters.

The way you, as parents and caregivers, treat your children is the way your children will treat others.

Effective teaching (discipline) should include several important things:

- A clear message

    Use simple, understandable language, words you know your child can understand. For example, "Billy, biting hurts your friend, Jamie. We never bite. We need to be kind and gentle to Jamie."

- Consistency

    Give your children the same clear message every time you need to correct them. It confuses them if you allow them to do something one day and not the next. Use simple words every time, such as "Hitting is never okay. If you hit someone, playtime will be over." You need to explain, in simple toddler language, why the behavior is not acceptable and what will happen if the child behaves that way again. Then, if it does happen again, you need to follow up with an appropriate consequence. *Follow-up is crucial to changing behavior.*

    Let's talk about appropriate consequences. We are, after all, talking about teaching very young children, twelve to thirty-six months old. A one-year-old is generally too young for typical effective toddler consequences; they don't yet have the ability to control much of their behavior. They simply react to what's going on around them. For the younger toddler, a firm "No" and then distraction or moving the child away from the problem works better. As they get closer to eighteen months, most toddlers begin to understand how consequences work

    Remember that the consequence needs to relate to the behavior you're trying to change. For example, Nick throws his toy truck at his brother. You explain that he should never throw toys, that if he throws the toy again, you will take it away. He does throw it again and you do take it away. This is an appropriate consequence and Nick will realize that if he throws the truck, he won't be able to play with it. You will also give him another chance the next day, explaining it all over again so that he understands. When he plays well with his little brother and doesn't throw the truck again, praise him for the good behavior. Children need positive reinforcement!

- A firm but gentle voice

Use a much more serious voice when you need to teach a lesson. Your children will soon learn to tell the difference in your tone of voice and know you want their attention. For example, "Ben, you must *always* stop and look for cars before you cross the street. Cars can't see you. They could hit you and hurt you."

- Carefully chosen words

> Children must know that they are loved no matter what they do, that it is their behavior that parents don't like and will not allow. This way, parents make it clear that they disapprove of the behavior, not the child.

Try to choose your words carefully. The words you use and the tone of voice you use can make a big difference in how your child reacts to the message. Your goal is to teach, not to shame.

Do tell your children you love them, even when they make mistakes. For example, "Jenny, I love you very much, but throwing sand is not okay. I know you'll try not to do that anymore."

- Removing a fun toy or privilege, if needed

For the older toddler (about two years and older), taking away something that is directly related to the behavior problem is important. If Max forgets to pick up his toys after playing, a good reminder would be to take those toys away for the day. When he realizes why they're gone, he will eventually learn to put them away to avoid losing them, even for a short time. If the behavior problem involves toys, then losing the toy should be the logical consequence. This simply means that you need to connect the behavior with the discipline. When Johnny and Alex continually fight during play, end their play for that day or separate them for a short time. Tell them they may try again to play together later, if they can play nicely. Giving toddlers another chance to try again helps them realize they can do better next time and learn from their mistakes.

- Taking immediate action

This can be a challenge for the parent or caregiver at times. It means you must be prepared to excuse yourself from the phone if necessary, pull the car off to the side of the road, or respond just as quickly in a restaurant as in your own

> **R**espond immediately when your child is misbehaving, in order for the child to learn from that mistake.

kitchen. It may be inconvenient, but it is very important to respond immediately. For example, if Cherise throws her cereal bowl on the floor, you could say, "Don't throw your food on the floor. If you do that, breakfast is over." If she does it again, take her down from her chair and end the meal. She will eventually learn that if she wants to eat, she can't throw her food.

- Talking about feelings, not just behavior

As toddlers begin to understand more words, they can also begin to understand the idea behind feelings—their own and other peoples' feelings. You can use this new understanding to role model how to express feelings. For example, "Molly, Daddy does not like it when you throw food. My job as your dad is to tell you it upsets me when you throw food, and to help you learn to stop doing that." This approach talks about real feelings as well as behavior.

Soon your toddlers will begin to talk about their own feelings, which is very important in being able to communicate well with others. If children are not able or not allowed to express how they feel, it will be extremely difficult to create trusting, loving relationships with others. Good, strong, long-lasting relationships are built on trust. Children need to be treated with love, respect, and trust so that they learn how to love themselves and others, how to treat others with kindness, and how to make good decisions.

Most often, people parent their children the way they were parented. It's very hard not to do to your own kids what was done to you, because we often copy the behavior of our own parents. The way you treat your children can affect the way your grandchildren are treated . . . and their children . . . and their children.

> **B**ehave the way you want your children to behave.

Being gentle, kind, and positive with your children will teach them to be gentle, kind, and positive toward others.

Learning: Child's Play Is Work

When that charming alarm clock rings every morning, you haul yourself out of bed and go to work or get your children ready for the new day. You have spent a lifetime learning all the things you know or do to survive in today's world. You started the day you were born and, surprisingly enough, approximately 90 percent of your brain development took place by the time you reached the age of five! So while you're busy going about your work every day, your toddlers are busy packing in the knowledge that they'll depend on for the rest of their lives.

Work and play are the same thing for toddlers. Children constantly learn through play. Albert Einstein said, "Play is the highest form of research." Looking at or listening to books, coloring or painting, creating shapes with clay and playing with toys of all kinds are the ways your little ones learn. They learn about stories, colors, and how different things feel in their hands (sticky clay; thick, wet finger paints; a smooth, round rubber ball; a hard, wooden block; a cold ice cube that's hard to hold one minute and slips through fingers the next). They learn about shapes and sizes and the difference between heavy and light or wet and dry. They learn to listen so they can follow a story that's being read to them, and they also learn to (try to) be patient and wait for the end of the story to find out what happens. Toddlers with less patience turn the pages two or three at a time or turn to the last page first to see how it ends! (I know adults who do that!)

Though the two little toddlers in my family had many different books to read, they always had their favorites. We read those books hundreds of times, and after they had heard them many times, they memorized parts or all of the stories. We would read the first part of the sentence and they would eagerly fill in the next word or line, or sometimes finish the whole story! They were so proud of themselves and we always praised them for knowing the words by heart.

Children love to hear exciting stories. Keep them simple at this age so your toddler can understand them. You can stop in the middle of your story, especially if you're making it up as you go along, and say, "What do you think happened next?" Most little ones love to make up their own stories or even add a small part to your story. Children also love to tell stories about themselves. It's a good way to learn what your young ones are thinking about and how they look at themselves

A great way to help your children learn to use their imagination is to teach them to tell their own stories.

and their place in the world. This is also a good age to start telling your children stories of your own childhood or your parents' or grandparents' lives. This way, they begin to get a sense of their family history and who they are. Parents can even put together a simple book about their toddler, with photos of the child doing fun activities, pictures of family and friends, and even drawings by the child. It's great fun to create a story to go along with the pictures. Toddlers love to read stories about themselves!

We're not talking about memorizing the Gettysburg Address here! Keep the challenge short and very simple. You don't want to frustrate your child on the first try. Toddlers love to be the center of attention and when they can repeat short rhymes or verses, everyone pays attention while they're "performing." Puppet shows (even with simple finger puppets) can stimulate creative thinking in older toddlers. We want our toddlers to enjoy using their brains and not just their fingers or hands and feet to learn new things. Reciting a very short poem helps them to think of themselves as smart and able to learn, and makes them feel good about themselves. Remember how you feel when someone compliments you—children feel the same way! Praise your children for learning new things and for trying hard, even (or especially!) when they don't succeed. Tell them you love them, and that you believe in them, and then watch them grow in self-confidence and self-esteem!

> **E**ncourage your children to explore, experiment, and learn new things. It can be fun to memorize a few words, a song, or a short poem.

Infants play with rattles and toys, but not really *with* other people. Toddlers watch others and respond to them, but the idea of playing in a situation where they learn to share toys or take turns or even play with the same toy at the same time as another person, is simply not something they can understand yet.

> **B**ecause toddlers believe that the world revolves around them, it takes a while for them to learn to play *with* others.

In addition to having an interest in toys, toddlers become more interested in people and what they do. Therefore, they begin to experiment with how to play differently. They begin to learn how something they do can affect what someone else does. For example, when Mom sits on the floor facing Julia and pushes a ball toward her, Julia may push the ball back. Then Mom pushes the ball toward her again. If she does not push the ball back, then Mom just sits there and so does the ball. . . and *that's boring*! So Julia pushes the ball back and it comes back to her. She begins to realize that she can make something happen; this is called "cause and effect" behavior. Quickly it becomes a game that Julia has learned and enjoys. The next time she wants to have fun, Julia can get the ball, sit down across from someone, and "play ball."

This activity is now a more complicated level of play than your little one has been used to. Instead of playing by herself, or near but not *with* someone else (this is called "parallel play"), Julia is now playing *with* someone else (this is called "interactive play") and she begins to see that it can be even more fun than playing alone, especially when the other person always lets her do just what she wants!

This is one of the first steps toddlers take toward becoming a cooperative member of their larger community. Use of the word "cooperative" is used loosely here—after all, we *are* talking about the toddler, who is not always known to be cooperative. In the example above, Julia begins to see herself as just one part of her world and not the center of it. This is no small step for a toddler. This means she begins to realize that she cannot control everything in her world, that her feelings are not the only ones that matter, and that she must sometimes wait her turn or share that beloved teddy bear with someone else for a little while. Think about this for a moment—think about how Julia must feel. Her whole life she has thought of herself as

> **S**he is beginning to realize that she may not be the most important person anymore, and that other people might count, too. This is a huge change in her view of herself and how she fits into her family and her community.

the queen bee. Suddenly, she begins to realize that others might be queen bees, too!

Parents and other adults need to encourage toddlers to see how they fit in as an equal part of this world. Whenever parents see their toddlers share toys, wait their turn, do what they're told without complaining, or show love, kindness, or generosity in any way, they should praise this behavior. That's how toddlers learn that what they're doing is correct and positive and they bask in the praise from their parents.

> Children love to be loved! They enjoy being told they're doing a good job, just like adults do.

This makes them proud of themselves, allows them to feel good about their behavior, and gives them a great reason to continue that positive behavior.

One of the most fascinating privileges of parenting is watching your little ones learn about themselves and life around them. As they realize that they are separate people from Mom and Dad, they begin to develop a strong curiosity about everything around them. This curiosity is a natural and very important part of the learning process.

Our job as parent or caregiver is to encourage that curiosity and therefore, help our kids learn as much as they can, as safely as they can.

> Discovering how things taste, feel, smell, look, and sound is an important "job" for a toddler.

One of the best ways to help children learn is to provide unstructured play every day. Let playtime be child-led, which means allowing your toddlers to explore their world and make choices about what they want to play with or how they want to play. At this age, the best toys are simple, like cardboard boxes, building blocks, books, balls, crayons, paints, puzzles, and other things that spark their imagination and learning as they play. Spending too much time in front of a screen (television, computers, tablets, electronic games) can seriously limit a child's creativity and imagination. The official American Academy of Pediatrics policy is *no screen time at all for children under the age of eighteen months.* Screen time for young children is associated with developmental and attention problems, aggressive behaviors, obesity, and other issues. Try to provide lots of different experiences for your little ones, such as playing with other children, making things by hand, or creating their own imaginary world of play indoors and outdoors, and watch and listen to what they enjoy doing. A child's play is his work! Mountains of research confirms that children learn best through play. Daily, unstructured play is a great way for your children to tap into their imagination and curiosity and to learn about the world around them.

Knowing that your toddlers must satisfy their need to investigate everything they see, you'll need to provide a safe place for them to explore. This means toddler-proofing your home (and yes, if possible, the homes your little one visits frequently). Since you know toddlers are not capable of deciding whether something is too hot to touch, too dangerous to play with, or too small to be put into their mouths without the chance of choking, it is your job to remove the things that could hurt your toddler. In *Raising Your Spirited Child*, author Mary Kurcinka suggests creating the "yes environment," a safe place where your child can freely explore without hearing "No, no" every two minutes. As soon as your child begins to crawl, take a good look around the entire house or apartment, since we never know where a small, curious child will begin to wander. Remove anything dangerous or valuable that is within reach or within climbing distance so there is less reason to limit your child's exploration.

You can also buy small plastic inserts for each of your electrical outlets, which plug the holes so your little one can't stick fingers or toys into them. They are not expensive, and they could save your child's life. They are available in your local hardware or department store.

This is usually important

> **C**heck your plants. Common houseplants can be poisonous if eaten, and whatever toddlers can reach will probably end up in their mouths.

until children are closer to three, when they begin to understand what they should and should not put into their mouths. Common flowers and plants such as azaleas, amaryllis, lily of the valley, rhododendron, hyacinth, and cyclamen are all toxic. Poinsettias (considered mildly toxic), holly, and mistletoe (considered toxic) are usually around during the winter holiday season and may be harmful if eaten.

Along with curiosity comes making messes. Now, wait a minute! I can see your eyes rolling back in your head, knowing the reputation toddlers have for making gigantic messes. But just take a minute to relax and think back . . . (*way* back, for some of us!) to the time when you were a child. You just may remember making some spectacular messes yourself at that age. After all, how can your children learn . . . *really* learn . . . about something, unless they get their fingers, faces, and toes right in there and take it apart, piece by piece, look it over, smell it, and sometimes even *taste* it?

> **Y**ou can get a list of poisonous plants from your poison control center; many of these centers also offer videos, poison safety guides, poison prevention packets, posters, and other educational materials, usually free.

How can they learn what it feels like to run through a mud puddle after a summer rain, unless they put some grubby old clothes on (or even a swimming suit) and run and splash through the nearest one they can find? How can kids see what they'd

> **H**ow can toddlers learn how mud feels, unless they take off their shoes and let it squish through their toes?

look like as a fancy, beautiful grown-up unless they take the make-up or markers they found and smear it all over their faces? And how can they ever learn to be a great cook unless they get a bowl out of the cupboard and, when no one is looking (they don't want to be interrupted!), throw in some flour and sugar, salt and pepper, a dash of ketchup, and maybe a few chocolate chips (after they've eaten most of the chips in the bag), just to see what it tastes like?

These are typical toddler messes (absolutely *not* limited only to this age group). Big, fat, gooey messes are not only fun to make, they get a lot of attention. Let's talk a little about the kind of attention these messes should get.

> **E**xperimenting and *doing* are the best way for toddlers to learn.

Digging inside things, tipping them over and dumping them out, taking things apart and putting them together, smelling, tasting, and touching things are all necessary parts of the investigation process for young children. You'll witness the joyful and creative side of your child if you let her experiment and not worry about the mess it might cause.

And then there's the very important toddler task of learning to feed themselves—often resulting in a huge mess on the high chair, on the floor, certainly on their clothes, or in their hair or ears. It takes practice to get food into their mouths, where it belongs. Just put a towel or newspaper on the floor under the high chair, give them a spoon and a short demonstration and then let them go for it!

Prepare yourself for a mess so you don't overreact. As your little one gets older, she'll get better at aiming for her mouth and will be very proud as you praise her for eating all by herself. And remember, table manners are not a toddler issue! You'll have plenty of time for that later.

Therefore, parents, please don't punish your toddlers for doing absolutely normal and important learning tasks such as those described

> **F**ind fun ways to allow your toddlers to try new things and learn about their world.

above. Of course, you need to set limits and guide them in order to avoid huge messes in the wrong place at the wrong time. The way you do this is to have your children ask you to help them experiment. But they won't ask you if they know you always say no when they want to try something new. Even though no might be your toddler's favorite word, don't let it be yours, too.

For example, you can encourage your little ones to learn by offering to help them mix a magic potion in the kitchen. That way you can control the kind and amount of ingredients that go into the brew and you can have fun together while your child learns about working in the kitchen. It does take some patience on your part, so choose a day when you have a little extra time and then have fun together!

Once again, try to *put yourself in your toddler's shoes* and remember that childhood lasts a very short time. Let them have fun and explore new things. Help them to develop their interests in many different things by encouraging them to ask questions, touch, watch, listen, smell, and sometimes, taste. I say "sometimes" because I vividly remember the day our eighteen-month-old son was playing in the grass while we pushed our daughter on the swing in the backyard. When I looked over at him, I saw him suddenly pull something long and thin out of his mouth and hold it up to look at. I dashed over to him and discovered that his newfound snack was a big, fat, shiny night crawler! Needless to say, I moved very quickly to wash out his mouth with water, and after my heart stopped beating visibly through my chest, I explained to my toddler, who couldn't figure out what all the excitement was about, that we don't ever eat worms!

> Try to remember to let your little ones enjoy the huge amount of learning that happens at this time in their lives. A little mud on clothes never clogged a washing machine, and a little soap on a child works wonders!

I was one of those "lucky" parents whose child was climbing everything in sight at a very early age. When our son was just twenty months old, I was working in the kitchen while he was playing with his toys in the living room. When I went to check on him, this is what I saw: my innocent young son had apparently seen a small toy on top of the television set. He had pushed our fairly large footstool over to the TV, climbed onto the stool, still couldn't reach the toy, and was heading for the top of the television set!

How he managed to do all of that without so much as a bump on the nose, I'll never know. I don't remember my feet touching the ground between the kitchen door and grabbing my child as he tried to climb onto the television set, but they must have, since it was about ten feet! Within the next sixty seconds, the footstool was moved into another room, where mountains would be a little harder to build.

(A note of caution: many families now have flat-screen TVs that weigh much less than older television sets, and are also much more likely to topple over on a toddler. Emergency rooms are seeing more and more serious injuries and even death in toddlers and young children from flat-screen TVs that have not been properly secured to the wall. Please check your TV and make sure it cannot fall on an innocent toddler walking by!)

> **I**f you remove everything that could hurt your toddlers or that they could damage, you'll be a more relaxed parent or caregiver and your little ones will have much more fun exploring and learning.

Remember, this is just for a short time in your life. As your toddlers get older, you can begin to teach them how to handle valuables carefully and how not to leave muddy footprints all over the rug. Put the good stuff away for a while and everyone will have more fun.

CHAPTER 3

The Jobs of the Twelve- to Thirty-Six-Month-Old

There are several "jobs" that your toddler will need to master during this general time period, but one thing needs to be perfectly clear to all parents: please don't panic if your little one doesn't follow this schedule exactly. Parents need to remember that every child is different. Don't expect Hannah to be toilet-trained by twenty-two months just because her sister Rachel was. Don't expect Anton to read at age three just because his brother James had read the whole Berenstain Bears series by then. Keep in mind that every child is unique—just keep encouraging your children and let them develop their own abilities and interests on their own timetable.

Speech

Take a moment to think back on that exciting day when the first real word burst forth from your baby's mouth. Often, it's "Mama" or "Dada" or some cute nickname for a brother or sister. When that day dawned at our house with our daughter, that long-awaited day when we could hear her say "Mama" or "Dada," we waited, ready to break into applause when our little darling finally called one parent by name, when out popped the word "Bop" . . . the name of our dog! Needless to say, we quickly learned who was "top dog" in her life.

Hearing those first words and realizing that your child really does understand the basic stepping-stones to the world of language and communication is very exciting. One of the toddler's jobs is to learn to talk. Your job is to talk very often with them, listen carefully, and encourage and praise your little ones enthusiastically when they make a new sound or say a new word.

Toddlers need to hear the words and sounds they make repeated back to them. This repetition helps them to understand how to take turns talking with another person. For example, if a toddler points at a cup and says something like "milk," Dad can say, "You would like a drink of milk?" Your

> The more excited the response your toddlers get, the more likely they will keep trying new sounds to impress you.

toddler then tries to repeat the word "milk." Sometimes parents won't understand what the child is saying, but an older sibling will translate. Eighteen-month-old Leif would repeatedly say "A-dee-doo" and point to the refrigerator. His parents couldn't figure out what he was trying to tell them. One morning, Leif's 4-year-old sister, Erin, said, "He wants a drink of juice!" Sure enough, Erin was right!

> "No," "mine," and "don't" are power words!

The single most preferred word over any other for this age group is probably "no." Coming in a close second is "don't," and another favorite is "mine." Until now, these words, particularly "no" and "don't," were used only by those around your little one, usually directed at your child.

Now, the tables have turned. When toddlers use these words, they get a reaction, positive or negative, depending upon the situation. Getting attention is important to children at every age, but particularly at this age, when they need lots of love and attention and will try almost anything to get it.

Whenever toddlers use these words, they are usually

> If you overreact, the lure of using these words becomes stronger, because they're getting a strong reaction.

expressing something negative and pushing you a little to see how far you'll let them go. What they're really doing is experimenting with something known as "cause and effect." They'll speak or act a certain way to see what will happen.

If you react calmly, your child may stop saying no and do what you ask... or not. Try to help this determined child to express these feelings by using simple words. For example, two- and-a-half-year-old Danny says, "No! I don't want to go to sleep!" when you tell him he needs to get ready for bed. In a calm voice, you could say, "You sound mad. It's okay to feel mad, but you still have to go to bed." Then follow your normal bedtime routine and put your toddler to bed. This may result in some kicking and screaming, but toddlers need to realize that parents are in charge, that they have been through every part of their normal bedtime routine, and now it's time to go to sleep.

Since this is just a phase that your child will pass through, remember not to take it personally when your toddler says no to you at every opportunity. Often, though it doesn't make sense (there may be *lots* of things that will happen during the toddler period that don't make sense), toddlers will sometimes say no when they really mean yes. For example, a friend was telling me that her two-year-old, Maria, was very frustrated one day. She wanted a piece of candy—*really* wanted it. (You'll find that when a toddler wants something, they never just sort of want it, they *really, really* want it!) She was fussing and reaching for the candy, but when Mom decided to give in and hand it to her, Maria said "No!" So her mom took it away and she immediately started screaming and reaching for it again.

> **I**f you give in just to quiet your children in public, they will continue to misbehave in public, knowing they will eventually get what they want.

Being reasonable and rational is not typically part of a toddler's daily goals. When your toddler wants one thing and you want another, frustration on both sides can escalate. You'll need to take a deep breath and face your child calmly. If parents lose their cool during times like these, it can make the situation much worse. Try to talk it through so you can teach your child the lesson you want her to remember.

The hardest part of this for parents and caregivers is not to give in when a child is making a scene, especially in public. In order for teaching to work, you must be consistent.

For example, every day when Andrea's mom picked her up from the childcare center, Andrea would ask to go to her friend's house. When her mother said no, Andrea would start crying and screaming. Andrea's mom would then tell Andrea that if she stopped behaving this way, she could have a special treat when they got home.

Unfortunately, this gave Andrea the idea that if she behaved badly, she could get a treat, just the opposite of what her mother was trying to teach her. If, on the other hand, when Andrea would misbehave, her mother would immediately tell her they were going home and that Andrea would be given a time-out, Andrea would have to pay a consequence for this behavior. Andrea would soon get the idea that if she misbehaved, she would have to be separated from everyone else, which she didn't like. Making sure a child experiences something they don't enjoy (without physical punishment) works well most of the time. Parents do have to try to be consistent—and that's often hard to do.

> **T**ry to keep reminding yourself that you are in charge, and that being firm and consistent when toddlers misbehave will pay off in the long run!

One last and very important part of teaching toddlers to behave properly is to compliment them when they do. This is extremely important in order to encourage good behavior. Children should be praised when they behave well in order to understand what is expected of them. Just as adults enjoy being complimented on a job well done, children must be treated the same way. "Catch them" being good and praise them for good behavior.

Think back to a compliment you received—didn't it make you feel good about yourself? Positive reinforcement is important for a child's self-esteem and encourages good behavior.

The way children feel about themselves, especially in the first three years, will affect them for the rest of their lives.

It's a challenge to parent a toddler! It requires massive amounts of patience, self-control, and understanding and often there is no easy answer. As you know, small children are not always rational human beings. Your son

> Encouragement, frequent hugs, and a daily "I love you" are as important to your children's self-confidence and self-esteem as food is to their bodies.

doesn't care, for example, that you're in a crowded store when he spots a shiny green gardening tool that he wants to play with. When you say no, he immediately throws a very loud, very embarrassing tantrum. You can't always compromise. This time you have to say no and your child is probably in no mood to hear the reasons for your decision: they're dangerous, you might get hurt, etc. Your best bet is to scoop him up and head for the door, or another area of the store, where you can try to calm him and yourself down in private.

Making sure your child understands the reason behind your decision is not always possible. *Kids need limits* and it is your responsibility to set reasonable ones and to be consistent in enforcing them.

Toddlers are famous for constantly pushing parents and caregivers to change the rules: two cookies instead of one, five more minutes on the swing, just one more book before bed . . . *"please, please, pleeeze?"* If you start giving

> All you can do sometimes is set limits and stick with your decisions.

in every time your toddler whines and pushes for more, you can create bigger problems. Little ones don't know when to stop and if they know you give in when they keep pushing, they will continue to push more and more. Set reasonable limits and stick with them—it will be much easier for everyone down the road. This is not to say that parents shouldn't compromise—flexibility is important to keeping the day rolling along as smoothly as possible, especially with an unpredictable toddler.

Speaking of compromise, this is one of the best lessons you can teach your children. The art of compromise is used daily throughout life—everyone's life. Little things, like eating fruit instead of cookies, are dealt with every day during the toddler stage.

> **A**dults compromise every day in other areas of their lives—children deserve the same flexibility.

For example, let them choose which color shirt, which pair of shoes, peas or carrots, meat or a piece of cheese, an apple or an orange, a walk or playtime in the park, reading a book or putting a puzzle together.

> **I**nstead of saying no every time your little ones want to do something that you disagree with, try giving them choices.

Teaching children how to make choices is very important. It's a great distraction when they want something they can't have and it reduces the number of times you have to say a flat no. It's also good training for future decision-making.

One more thing: give yourself a break. Parenting is a tough job and nobody is perfect. If you make it through a tough day and you've managed to stay calm and fairly reasonable, take credit for it. Pat yourself on the back and take time to feel good about it. After all, parents need praise, too!

Learning to Share

The focus of two-year-old Erin's world is herself. No one else is as important, no one's feelings matter as much, no one else's needs or desires should be satisfied before her own. She does not yet understand that she is simply a part of the enormous world around her, not the center of it. In child development jargon, this is referred to as "egocentrism."

That is why it's so difficult for Erin to wait her turn, to share her toys, or to take no for an answer from anyone, especially from toddlers her own age who are looking at life from the same "I come first!" viewpoint. That is also why we need to teach toddlers that everybody is important!

These lessons are absolutely crucial stepping-stones to becoming aware of themselves as separate people, as well as their role as an important member of their family and their world.

Lessons such as how to share, how to be kind, and how to be patient are usually very difficult to teach a toddler because until they are nearing or even past the age of three, these ideas are simply too complicated for them to understand. But keep teaching, parents.

At this age, not sharing toys is very common, so to avoid some of these tussles, try to have similar kinds of toys available for toddlers when they play together. However, having a little pal yank a toy out of his or her hands is one of the ways a toddler begins to learn how to use words and how to give and take (literally). Try not to jump in every time your little ones argue over a toy. Wait to see if they can work it out themselves. Obviously, if someone is about to be clobbered with a toy airplane, you have to step in. But use this opportunity, called a "teachable moment," to teach both toddlers about sharing. You might say, "Emma, it's time to share the toy with Elli for a while. We'll set the timer. When it rings, Elli will give

When you show little ones over and over how to trade or share toys, it begins to make more sense to them. It takes lots of repetition and patience on the part of the parent before the whole idea begins to make a difference in the way toddlers play together.

you the toy to play with. When you share, you'll both be able to play with the toy."

Try not to expect too much of a two-year-old in terms of sharing. Closer to age three or even older, when toddlers have more words and more experience, they can begin to really understand what it means to share. They don't necessarily *like* it, but they slowly begin to understand it, especially when it's *their* turn to have the toy!

Take them to the park, for a walk, to the wading pool, or to the library, where they can play with somebody else's things. It's always best to consider just what we can expect our little ones to handle and to plan activities with this in mind.

> Try to plan a variety of activities where toddlers won't need to share their toys or play closely together for long periods. Avoiding the problem works best!

Toilet Training

Anyone who's ever raised a child usually has at least one great toilet training story to tell and that's because this process is often a big challenge for both you and your toddler. It is very important to treat this period in your toddler's life with patience and sensitivity. It's a major change for very young children to learn to go into the bathroom when they have to urinate or have a bowel movement (BM) instead of just letting go into their diaper.

Certain things must take place before your toddler is ready to be toilet trained.

Since it is your child who needs to eventually learn to use the bathroom, it is your child who must

> This process usually takes several weeks to several months to complete for daytime control. Nighttime control often takes longer.

signal an interest in beginning the process. You, as parent or caregiver, need to look for clues from your little one to know when the proper time to start training has arrived. If you begin before your child is ready, it can be very difficult for everyone and may ultimately take much longer to accomplish.

> **I**t doesn't happen just because you are tired of changing diapers—it's your *child* who must be ready before you both will be successful at toilet training.

Toddlers must be physically ready to hold urine or feces before they are ready to be trained. To be "ready" is quite complicated. Your toddlers need to recognize the feeling of needing to urinate, know what it means, not give in to the reflex to just "let go," stop what they are doing, get into the bathroom, pull down their diaper or underwear, sit down on the toilet, and then, and only then, let go into the toilet. Whew! No wonder it takes a long time to learn!

Toddlers are usually successful during the daytime hours long before they will be able to hold their urine overnight, which is not only a much longer period of time to be dry, but during sleep, they're often unable to feel that their bladder is full.

Two-and-a-half-year-old Elijah began to show interest in what his parents and brothers did in the bathroom, and he began to ask questions about

> **W**atch for clues, such as your child staying dry for several hours at a time, or waking up with a dry diaper either after a nap or overnight.

going to the bathroom in the toilet. His parents answered his questions and encouraged him to try. It's very unlikely that Elijah will be able to urinate whenever he wants to at first. It is the rare child who is trained overnight . . . but someone will always tell you that they know of a child who never had an accident from the first time he used the toilet! Try not to get your hopes up—that is literally a one-in-a-million kid! It rarely happens that easily.

Parents can expect that this process will take several weeks to several months and will often be much longer before their toddler stops having an occasional accident. This is the average amount of time parents can expect—remember that every child is different! Allow toilet training to take as much time as your child needs. Try very hard not to expect more from your toddlers than they can actually give you.

> **Y**our own attitude is absolutely critical to the success or failure of the toilet training process.

It will help tremendously for everyone involved to approach this challenging process positively. If, for example, Elijah wants to try sitting on the toilet, he will need either a small, toddler-sized toilet seat that fits inside the rim of the toilet or better yet, a small potty chair all his own, which sits on the floor of the bathroom and is comfortable to sit on. Elijah needs to be comfortable in order to sit there longer than a few seconds, so he needs a little stool for his feet if he must stay perched on an adult-sized toilet. This should be a positive experience, not a scary one!

Elijah's parents need to approach this process with patience and flexibility. If Elijah happens to have a BM in his potty chair once, it may just be luck. One success doesn't mean that he now understands exactly what to do. The process has just begun. Whenever Elijah urinates or has a BM in the potty chair, he should be praised! It makes him feel good about himself, and makes him want to do it again, just to hear his parents tell him how proud they are of him and what a big boy he is.

> **T**oddlers should always be complimented when they are successful, but never punished for having an accident.

Another toddler red alert:

Your little ones are just learning a new and *very difficult* process: learning to listen to their bodies and respond quickly. It simply doesn't always work as planned. Sometimes toddlers are too involved in play to be aware of the urge to go to the bathroom.

Sometimes, when they have to urinate and they happen to be playing with or in water, they'll wet their pants. In fact, that's a great way to get your toddlers to urinate when you would like them to—assuming they haven't just been to the bathroom. Put them on the potty chair and turn on the water to a slow trickle and have them listen to the water sounds. If a child has to go at all, this often works. Sometimes they realize too late that they have to go, and they don't make it in time. Be patient. Practice makes perfect—*lots* of practice, usually!

Toddlers are able to learn only as much as their age level will let them learn. These are little, tiny human beings who cannot control much of what happens to them.

WARNING: accidents can trigger anger in a parent, especially when you have just dressed your toddlers in their best clothes for a special occasion and are headed out the door! Be very aware that when you begin toilet training, it's often a long and usually challenging teaching process. Try to stay patient and calm and very encouraging if you expect your little ones to learn anything, because it is not a fun process for them, either! Once again, *think about how your toddler feels.* You are now asking this tiny person to take responsibility for something that happens to them, without much warning, several times a day and at night, too! It doesn't even make sense to them, and everyone is making a big deal about it! And you're expecting cooperation! It doesn't sound like much fun, does it?

> The toilet training process is usually a long-term learning situation—please don't expect it to be over quickly. It's a complicated and completely new behavior you are trying to teach.

A wonderful example of how your toddler needs to feel about learning to go to the bathroom is Hannah's story. One day, their dog had an accident on the floor. Two-year-old Hannah walked over to him, patted him on the head and said, "That's okay, Scootie, accidents happen. No biggie." Clearly, her wise parents had given Hannah the message that toilet training is a learning process and that accidents are nothing to be ashamed of. It's the very rare child who never has an accident during this challenging process.

You are in this together! If you punish your toddlers or get angry when they have accidents, or if you're impatient when they want to go to the restaurant restroom five minutes after the last trip, when they didn't urinate, it will take much longer to convince them that they need to learn to do this. Use a positive and encouraging approach—take lots of deep breaths, count to ten, keep smiling through gritted teeth, always take an extra set or two of clothes along, and you'll make the whole process shorter and easier. Attitude is everything here!

If you are lucky enough to have a toddler who has a BM on a regular schedule (this is rare), say, right after breakfast every morning, you may want to try giving your child a favorite book to look at while sitting on the potty chair after breakfast. Sometimes, if Lady Luck is in your corner, you can time it so your toddler has a BM in the potty chair. If this happens, praise your child. And then realize that it was probably your timing and not your toddler's understanding that made it happen!

If you expect too much too soon during the toilet training process, it may backfire. Your little one may just refuse to cooperate at all. Remember, you can control most things in this

> Forcing toddlers to sit on the potty chair for long periods until they urinate or have a BM is not effective. Just as *you* cannot be forced to go to the bathroom on demand, neither can your child!

child's life, but you cannot control when your toddler urinates or has a BM—and your child learns very fast that this is an area where he or she has some control!

When Katie was a two-year-old, it seemed as though she knew that her dad was a behavioral pediatrician who helped other parents with their children's problems. Each time she began to show an interest in urinating in the toilet and Mom and Dad got excited (cartwheels and headstands!), she would stop, as if to say, "I'm not especially interested in doing this just so *you* can be happy!" Her parents knew that it wasn't unusual for the process to drag on until a child is well over three years old. So they would drop the issue for a month or so and then try again. They also bought a book on toilet training that soon became her favorite (*Toilet Learning* by Allison Mack). It had pictures of various people on the toilet. "Grandma goes to the toilet, police officer goes on the toilet, doctor goes on the toilet," she would say from memory. Excitedly her dad would say, "And Katie goes to the toilet?" "No, Daddy!" was her answer. In fact, to show them how she really felt, she actually urinated on the book before she ever went on the toilet! The good news was that when the time was right, it was right, and the toilet training happened very quickly—but not until *Katie* was ready! If you make this process one of punishment and frustration instead of a new experience that will make your children feel proud whenever they're successful, they may decide to turn the tables on you. Your little one may either hold it when in the bathroom, or let loose when you are nowhere near a restroom! You need to work *together* on this one!

One parent told me he put a potty chair in the bathroom when their toddler was just a year old. The idea was to get the child used to seeing the chair, but not to expect him to actually learn to toilet train that early. When it came time to begin potty training, it was not a strange new idea because he had seen it in the bathroom for months.

Books and small toys often work well when you want your little ones to sit on the potty chair. If they refuse, tell them you just want them to try, and that they can play with their special bathroom toys while they do. You may want to keep a couple of special toys or books just for use in the bathroom, as a reason for your toddlers to go into the bathroom to try. Allowing them to sit there as long as they are comfortable doing that, and not forcing them to stay when they want to get up (even if they haven't left anything in the potty chair) is a positive, effective approach. Thank your little ones for trying and suggest that maybe next time they'll be able to go.

> **M**ake it a fun challenge and keep it positive!

Once again, a little treat for a job well done may be in order here. M&M's worked well in our family (but more nutritional treats are recommended!). We would put our daughter on the potty chair and when she decided she was finished, if she actually urinated or had a BM, we would give her one or two M&M's after she washed her hands. As she got better at it, we gradually reduced the treats and praised her instead and eventually she was going just for the praise and forgot about the candy. But we had to give her the treat long enough so that she understood the connection between going to the bathroom and getting the treat. Try to very gradually reduce the reward, or you may find yourself starting all over again!

Big boy or big girl underwear is also a great reason for your little one to stay dry. Once your toddlers are not wearing diapers during the daytime anymore, they'll want to tell everyone all about their big boy or big girl underwear . . . and probably show them, too! If you've reached the point where your toddlers are staying dry for at least a few hours during the day, you may want to reward them by taking them to the store and letting them choose which special underwear they want to buy. These are not expensive, and it really does help toddlers to remember to try to get into the bathroom on time so they can keep their new underwear dry. WARNING: always try to remember to take along a couple extra sets of clothing, wet wipes, and a plastic bag whenever you leave the house. This will help to reduce tension when there is an accident, allowing everyone to treat it as a natural part of the toilet-training process. Accidents *will* happen!

As with any behavior change, it helps to give your child incentive to change. One parent squirted a few drops of what he called "magic potty colors" (food coloring!) into the toilet, which his child loved to watch swirling down the toilet!

There are very logical times during the day when you should have your toddlers try to go to the bathroom: as soon as they wake up in the morning, after meals, before and after naps, before bedtime, and just before they go to play in the next door

> **R**emember, when there is an accident, take a deep breath, try not to get angry, and remind yourself that this is definitely a normal part of the whole process of toilet training.

neighbor's new wading pool! As you both keep trying, your toddlers will gradually get the idea, especially when they're successful and you reward them with praise or a treat. This is a great time to show unconditional love for your child—you still love and support them whether or not they are successful.

Just suggest to your toddlers that they need to try to get into the bathroom *before* there is an accident, that they're a big girl or big boy now, and that they can try again next time. Then change them into dry clothes and move on to something else.

Try to remember that your toddler wants to be successful and to please you. Help them to feel good about themselves by keeping this challenging process positive.

Bed-wetting is completely normal. It's really too early to expect your toddler to stay dry during the night. Many (but definitely not all) toddlers learn to be dry during the day around the age of three, some children earlier. Staying dry at night, however, often happens between three and four. Unless your child wakes up dry several mornings in a row, it's better to just concentrate on the daytime toilet training until around age three. Again, every child is different!

Some young toddlers often do not understand why, after they have a BM and you praise them for producing it, you then want to flush it down the toilet. Jayson, at two-and-a-half, didn't want to flush the toilet after he had a BM. He wanted to look at it and even touch it to see what it felt like. Parents, a reaction like this is just normal curiosity for a toddler. Jayson's parents did let him look at it (forget the touching part!) before they disposed of it. But they explained that it was something his body no longer needed, and that's why they flush it down the toilet. Jayson fussed a great deal the first few times they flushed the toilet. If this happens, don't flush right away. Let your toddlers wash their hands and get them involved in play in another

> **P**ay attention to the clues your own child is giving you, and try not to compare your toddler with any other toddler. Different children are on different schedules.

part of the house; then go back and flush later. Let them get used to the idea slowly. It's a very strange idea for your toddler to get used to and it means more to some children than to others. *Again, try to focus on how your child must be feeling!* By trying to put yourself in your child's place, and remembering that it is very difficult to master this complicated process, it will be easier to be more patient.

Not all children have daily BMs. If your child doesn't have a BM every third day, has large or painful BMs, or seems to be trying to hold back BMs, you should see your doctor. This may be a sign of a form of constipation that needs medical treatment before your child can be toilet trained successfully.

Expect occasional accidents—even after you're *sure* they've learned how to control when and where they go to the bathroom—especially if you don't take them seriously when they say they have to go!

For example, you and your three-year-old son are in the mall. It's the annual Daisy Sale and the store is jammed with wild-eyed bargain hunters. After searching madly for an hour, you've found just what you wanted, for even less than you expected, and are waiting in a *very* long line to check out. Suddenly, your little one says, "Mommy, I have to go to the bathroom." (We suggest you teach your child to say "go to the bathroom" instead of "go pee-pee or poop." Toddlers need to be taught the correct words to describe what they need . . . and it truly sounds a lot more civilized, doesn't it?) You still have five people ahead of you. Unfortunately, you also have nine people behind you, and you know that if you take the time to take your son to the restroom, it will take you forty-five minutes longer to get home, and you'll be very late picking up your daughter at school.

So! What's a parent to do? Stall! You look down at your now-wiggling toddler and say, "Just a couple minutes longer, honey. You can hold it, can't you?" You then try to distract your child by showing him some fascinating sweater hanging on the rack next to you, hoping desperately that he'll forget, just for ten minutes, that he has to go the bathroom. Thirty seconds later, your toddler is jumping around from one foot to the other, holding his crotch and whining, "Maaaaaamaaaaa! I have to go *right now! Right, right now!*" You are now just *two* people from the front—*surely* he doesn't have to go *that* badly! "Just one more minute, honey. I know you can wait just a *teensy* bit longer!" As you look down at your frustrated, wriggling, red-faced toddler, you suddenly see him relax and a look of great relief spreads over his face. With growing fear, your eyes drop to the floor, where a telltale yellow pool is forming slowly around his scuffed, red sneakers . . .

Yup, you've blown it . . . you just expected more of your toddler than he could give you and he tried to tell you! Your only solution now is to dig out all the scraps of Kleenex from the bottom of your purse, wipe up as much as you can off the floor (with all eyes now on *you*, of course!), and leave as quickly as possible. After you're home and you're both washed and dried, sit down with your son and apologize.

Tell him that what happened was not his fault and that you know he tried to tell you that he needed to go to the bathroom. Tell him that you made a mistake and waited too long. Again, *think of how he must be feeling*—he did what you taught him to do; he told you when he had to go to the bathroom! Then praise him for telling you that he needed to go to the bathroom and tell him you will take him right away next time. He needs to know that it was not his fault.

> **O**ne of the most effective ways for you to teach your child that nobody is perfect is to let him know that adults make mistakes, too.

Everyone who has raised a child has stories like this to tell, and for better or worse, we all learn from them. When you've spent all that time training your child, and he does what you tell him, respond right away, because many times, your little one won't tell you he has to go until the very last minute. As he gets older, he'll be able to recognize the signs sooner. Be patient and it will all fall into place eventually.

CHAPTER 4

Typical Toddler Topics

The Food Thing

Until my son, AJ, was two and a half, he would eat almost every vegetable that was put in front of him. Suddenly, one day he refused to eat peas. The next day it was corn, and soon, he wouldn't even look at a green bean, much less eat it! Of course, we had no idea what brought on this sudden change, but we realized that, somehow, we had to sneak some vegetables into this now former veggie-lover.

His dad and I wanted him to know that he needed to eat fresh fruits and vegetables as part of his daily food. We asked him what kind of vegetables he liked and he said, "Carrots with stuff on them." After we asked him to show us what the "stuff" was, AJ led us to the refrigerator and pointed to the dill dip. We soon discovered that dip (any dip or any of the salad dressings that he liked) was the magic solution to the "How do I get my kid to eat vegetables?" problem. As long as he was allowed to dunk his vegetables into a dip or dressing that he liked (and I do mean "dunk"—one time he actually used the carrot as a spoon to shovel dip into his mouth!), he would eat plenty of

> **A**lthough these little ones are very smart, sometimes we need to outsmart them to keep everyone healthy and happy. Food is one area where disguises can work.

them. His dad also gave AJ fruit yogurt as a dip for fresh fruit and he loved it. Be sure to check out the ingredients in the salad dressing or dip you use—they can be very high in fat and sugar.

For example, when you're making pancakes, pour the batter from a measuring cup slowly onto the hot pan in the shape of an animal, a car, or a heart. (Trust me, this is easier than it sounds and you don't have to be a brilliant artist to do it. Just remember to pour slowly.) Or, instead of serving a plain pancake, decorate it with a happy face made with berries and apple or banana slices. For sandwiches, cut pieces of cheese or bread into different shapes, just to make the food more fun and exciting to eat. Kids get bored with the same old food, just like adults do! You can also shred carrots or zucchini into hamburgers or toss a handful of wheat germ into cookie batter—the kids will get a nutritional boost and you can avoid a fight with your child.

Remember to be aware of foods that a toddler might choke on: raw carrots, hot dogs or other meats, grapes, or cherry tomatoes that the child might put into his mouth whole. Make sure to cut these foods and any others into small pieces to prevent choking and sit with your child while he eats.

Food is a constant source of worry for parents and caregivers. Are they getting enough, the right kinds, a balanced diet every day? If they don't eat one day, or if they're sick and don't eat well for three days, will it harm their health? If your children are sick and not eating, watch them closely. Make sure that they get enough to drink, which is much more important than food for a couple of days. If they refuse to drink liquids, try Kool-Aid or popsicles while they're sick if you can't get them to drink water, milk, or fruit juice. Hydration is critical when your child has a fever.

Generally speaking, if your

Keep popsicles in the freezer for emergencies—popsicles work well to help reduce swelling for a mouth or lip injury or to hydrate your child.

child doesn't eat for more than two days, it's wise to get advice from your health care provider.

Let's talk about milk for a moment. Milk is important for Vitamin D and calcium, but toddlers who drink too much milk aren't hungry for nutritious food that their bodies need for healthy development. A toddler who still carries a bottle around during the day may be filling up on fluids, resulting in less appetite for healthy food. By weaning your toddler early to a cup instead of a bottle, you can more easily control the amount of milk or juice your child drinks. Some breast-feeding moms wean the child right to the cup and prevent the bottle problem completely.

Juice is another issue to consider. The general rule is to limit juice to four ounces per day. Juice often contains as much sugar as soda, which is not recommended for young children. Toddlers who are allowed to drink juice out of a bottle during the day can get way too much sugar in their daily diet. (It's very easy to dilute juice by adding water, which most toddlers don't notice.) The American Academy of Pediatrics encourages parents not to put babies and toddlers to bed with a bottle at naptime or at night, as the sugar from either milk or juice sits in the child's mouth and can cause cavities, while also adding many calories to their daily diet. Giving your toddlers a drink of water before a nap or bedtime and teaching them to go to sleep without a bottle helps to assure better overall health.

Let's touch on pacifiers for a moment. Pacifiers are meant to soothe newborns and young babies who have a strong need to suck and limited ways to soothe themselves. Toddlers and older kids have many ways to calm themselves—distraction with a toy or book, going outside, playing games, having a healthy snack, etc. It's a very good idea to gradually wean your young toddler off the pacifier and teach her new ways to cheer herself up. Parents whose toddlers have become literally attached to their pacifier (some parents pin the pacifier to the shirt of the child) can tell stories about toddlers erupting into a tantrum at the park or grocery store because they've lost their pacifier. This scene can be prevented by teaching your little one different ways to calm down, so that there is no longer a need for a pacifier (or bottle).

Since food is such a common issue for parents, there have been many studies done to try to determine what is important and what's not for a toddler. Generally speaking, if you offer a wide variety of foods to your little ones—fresh fruits and vegetables, milk and juice (100% juice with no sugar added), bread (whole wheat or multigrain are great nutritional choices), rice or noodles (brown rice or wheat-based noodles are a good option), beans, meat or fish, and dairy products—they should get a fairly well-balanced diet. If your child eats a well-balanced daily diet, they shouldn't need a multivitamin. If you're not sure your toddler is getting the proper nutrition, please discuss it with your health care provider.

Toddlers certainly don't eat everything they should every day (neither do adults), and there will be days when you think they'll starve and days when they're constantly hungry. But, over several days, if you present a good variety of fresh food, avoid preservatives, and try to limit the amount of sugar and fats they eat, toddlers will generally get what they need. But don't give up on the foods you know they need for good health. Continue to offer them periodically—as we know, toddlers are very good at changing their minds!

> So! About this food thing? Relax a little! Just as adults prefer to eat a certain kind of food one day and not the next, children have similar preferences. They may not eat much at all one day, or even for two days, but eventually they'll get hungry and make up for it.

It's not a good idea to force a child to eat exactly what you eat every day. This is definitely not to suggest that you make a separate meal for your little ones. Instead, try to offer them choices. For example, if they don't like pork chops, offer them a piece of cheese instead. They'll get the protein either way and you avoid a fight, which could spoil the meal for everyone.

But keep offering them new foods so they become used to trying new things. Young kids often learn to eat the foods they reject the first few times.

Remember to try to *look at it from your child's perspective*. Children have food preferences, just as adults do. One important thing to remember is not to put too much food on your child's plate and then expect him to eat every bite. Start with small portions—child-size portions. You can always add more food if your child would like more.

> **E**ncourage your toddlers to try new foods, but don't expect them to like or to eat everything you put in front of them.

If you make a big deal out of everything they put into their mouths, they'll become aware that they have power over you and can get lots of attention if they refuse to eat. Approach the situation positively, try new things, and let them make some choices about which vegetable to eat or whether to have a piece of cheese or beans or peanut butter (all good sources of protein) instead of meat. Use your imagination to steer clear of confrontations about food and mealtimes can be something you look forward to instead of a time to dread. This way, everyone wins.

Imagination: Magic and Fantasy

Sit back for a moment and close your eyes; allow yourself to think back to your earliest memories of childhood. Now, who are you? Yes. *Who are you?* A princess in a long flowing gown (your mom's old prom dress, perhaps)? Superman, with a big red "S" printed on a dish towel and thrown over your shoulder? A cowboy with a clothesline hooked onto your belt, ridin' your horse toward the OK Corral for a little bronco-bustin'? Or maybe you were a bit more tame when it came to imagining who you were going to "be" each day. Maybe you were a teacher, a firefighter, a truck driver, or somebody's mom or dad. It usually didn't matter who you became when you played, but it was a very important part of your life as a toddler.

For one thing, a fantasy world is more fun than everyday life, and secondly, the toddler can be in control of what happens there—and for a little one who is always told what to do, what to eat, and when to sleep, this is a welcome change.

> **I**magination plays a huge part in everyday life at the toddler stage, especially after about two and a half years of age—toddlers sometimes prefer the fantasy world to the real one.

A toddler's imagination is truly an amazing thing. Ana can be an airline pilot one minute and a crane operator the next. There are no boundaries in her fantasy world. She can be either sex, big or small, very sweet or terribly mean. She, and she alone, makes the decisions in her imaginary world.

Many toddlers create imaginary friends, particularly if they are the oldest child or the only child in the family. This way, if children can't have a friend over and Mom and Dad are busy, they still have someone to play with.

My two-and-a-half-year-old daughter, Erica, all by herself in her room or in the back seat of the car, would often chatter away happily. When asked who she was talking to, she would always say, "Condo-wondo, Mee-um See-um, and my sisters." Where she came up with those particular people we will never know! But that's part of the reason toddlers do have imaginary friends: to have something special that belongs only to them, to call upon whenever they choose. Don't worry that your kids are lonely or that they feel neglected just because they have an imaginary friend. Many busy and happy toddlers create imaginary friends to make their world more interesting.

> **H**aving an imaginary friend is fun and a very normal thing for a toddler to do.

How many times have you found yourself daydreaming, imagining yourself on a tropical island, perhaps sipping an icy cold drink while you sit in the shade of a huge palm tree, listening to the waves gently lap against the white, sandy beach while a cool breeze blows gently against your face? Sounds nice! This is called "fantasy" and it allows you to escape your everyday life for a while and imagine yourself some place much more fun and exciting. (Unfortunately, the scene above is usually fantasy for most young parents!) After you've enjoyed a few relaxing minutes on the beach, reality suddenly strikes and you force yourself to go back to work or studying or cleaning. You know you weren't really on a beach—you were there in your imagination only.

> **W**hen toddlers watch violent cartoons, in which someone hits another on the head with a frying pan, or blows another up with a stick of dynamite, or pushes another out of a speeding car and that person always gets up and walks away, they think it's real.

This is a major difference between an adult and a toddler: toddlers cannot tell the difference between fantasy and real life. That's why you, as parent or caregiver, need to do it for them.

This is another toddler red alert! When two-year-old Juan sits in front of a television or movie screen and watches a show or cartoon, it is real to him. When he sees someone hit or shoot or hurt another person on screen, he thinks it's real. Not only does violence on television or a movie frighten Juan, it also teaches him a lesson in behavior, the worst possible behavior. Remember: children copy what they see.

> **S**tudy after study has shown that children can be negatively affected by watching violence on TV, movies, and cartoons.

When Juan watches *Superman*, he may tie a towel over his shoulders and pretend to fly off to rescue someone. That's harmless enough—unless, of course, he "flies" off a window ledge two stories high!

As long as they see it happen, it's real to them. They are likely to try to copy that behavior because toddlers are copycats.

Often, their behavior imitates the violent behavior they have just seen—not always, and not with every child, but frequently. Children can develop a passive attitude toward violence, which means that after seeing it a lot, they don't even react to it anymore. Therefore, they don't react to it as being wrong, they just accept it as a normal part of life.

They may see extremely harmful behavior and they will learn from it. If you take the time to sit down with your children to watch at least part of what they're watching, you can judge for yourself whether it's good for your child to watch.

> **P**arents need to protect little ones from violence in their lives—real violence and fake violence in cartoons, TV, and movies—because they are both the same to a toddler.

Better yet, you can avoid the problem. The American Academy of Pediatrics recommends *no screen time for children under age eighteen months (except for video-chats)*, and for children between eighteen and twenty-four months, limiting screen time to one hour or less per day. They also recommend choosing only quality programs and watching with your child. Please tell your older children that they, too, need to protect their little brother or sister from watching scary shows. The whole family must be aware of the harm that can be done to small children, and older children, as well, by watching violent shows. Toddlers are innocent and sensitive little beings who need to be protected.

Thumb-sucking

Thumb-sucking is another toddler issue that comes up frequently. Kids vary tremendously in how or even whether they suck their thumbs. Some babies start sucking their thumb as soon as they can find it—witnessed on a monitor by soon-to-be moms and dads through the miracle of ultrasound! Some children never show the slightest interest in it.

Often parents worry that their little ones will never stop sucking their thumbs, or that they'll somehow interfere with the proper development of their mouths or teeth.

The usual pattern of thumb-sucking starts sometime during the infant stage and ends sometime between three and five years, but again, this varies from child to child. A general recommendation is to treat thumb-sucking as a normal part of your child's development. Toddlers often choose to suck their thumbs because it is one way they can comfort themselves. Thumbs are always available (not necessarily *clean*, but available) and within reach whenever needed. When toddlers are tired, sad, lonely, frightened, nervous, or especially when their parents aren't around, they are able to make themselves feel better by sucking. Sucking is one of the most important survival instincts babies possess. Even at the newborn stage, babies use sucking not only for eating, but also for comforting themselves when they're unhappy.

> **M**ost children's dentists agree that thumb-sucking before age five is not likely to cause dental problems. However, if thumb-sucking continues after permanent teeth begin to come in, the result may be crooked teeth.

> **M**ost children are aware that thumb-sucking is accepted as something "babies" do, so by the time they enter late preschool or kindergarten, they want to be seen as a "big kid" and stop sucking all by themselves.

Because sucking has been so important to them, it is sometimes difficult for toddlers to give it up as they get older.

If your little one is still sucking his thumb after about five years old, there are some things you can do to encourage him to stop.

The most important thing to remember here is that any kind of physical punishment or shaming words are not the way to change behavior, especially something as natural as sucking.

Setting up a daily chart and allowing your toddler to put a sticker on each morning or afternoon they spend without thumb-sucking, followed by a little reward when two or more days in a row have stickers, can be very effective. Always start with small expectations and then very slowly increase them to give kids every chance to succeed and feel good about themselves. Praising toddlers and telling them how grown-up they look when they don't suck their thumbs can also help.

> Giving toddlers a positive reason to stop sucking their thumb is the most effective method for behavior change.

Most kids give up thumb-sucking on their own before the age of five, so don't panic. Your child just might be one of them!

Favorite Blanket or Toy

At some point during babyhood or toddlerhood, many kids choose a special toy, often a doll, stuffed animal, or special blanket, as their favorite. This is another normal and natural part of being a toddler.

Your little ones may take their favorite toy to bed with them, to the park, or to the local ice cream store. Some little ones need only to hold their special toy occasionally when they're feeling sad or tired; others won't let it out of their sight.

> Keeping something that they know and love very close to them can help toddlers feel more comfortable and secure, especially in a new or strange situation.

We've all heard horror stories about going on a family trip and forgetting, of all things, your toddler's favorite, can't-go-any-place-without-it, must-have-it-to-breathe toy or blanket. The problem usually is that you don't discover you've left it behind until you're at least fifty miles from home and there's no turning back. (Actually, this can happen during trips across town on the bus!) Often, this discovery results in hysterical shrieking and crying, accompanied by statements such as, "I really, *really* need my teddy . . . *right now!*" "I won't take a nap 'til I get my binkie!" "Wa-a-a-h! I want my snuggles! I want my snuggles!" This situation generally results in great distress and chaos, at least for a short time. Something to keep in mind is that you and your child will survive this event. You might want to try any or all of the following:

Most importantly, try to stay calm. As mentioned before, if you get upset along with your child, you may lose your chance to effectively control what happens. First, encourage your child to express her feelings. It's not helpful right now to tell Gina that she's "too old" to need a favorite toy or blanket—she needs you to understand that she's sad and missing the comfort she gets from her favorite toy. As they get older, children gradually grow out of needing their toy or blanket, but it usually takes time. Sometimes, though rarely, it happens suddenly, when the last teensy piece of blanket disintegrates or the toy is actually lost. At this young age, however, you need to be understanding and help to make it better somehow.

If Gina is still upset, try changing the subject (sometimes, this actually works!). Point out the window at something (in our family, it was usually good old Midwest farmland) and say, "Oh, Gina, look at the pretty cow . . . what does the cow say?" Then praise her for saying, "Moo!" and go on to all the other animal sounds she knows. Sometimes you can get her to think about something else until you can figure out a way to solve the problem. Sometimes you can't—in that case, try the following:

Books can be the magic answer at times like these, especially if you're already in the habit of reading books to your toddler and it's a happy activity for both of you. (Remember that

> **R**eading good children's books together gets the highest possible approval rating as a valuable and fun activity in almost *any* situation!

reading, scribbling, and talking with your toddler will help his or her brain develop; a love of reading books helps your child to become a better reader and writer later.) Pick up one of Gina's favorite books and start reading out loud. Very often, your toddler will stop fussing or crying in order to hear the story.

Or grab another toy out of the bag of stuff that you've brought along.

> **B**ring along lots of things for your toddler to play with—it will make the whole trip go more smoothly.

Sometimes kids have more than one favorite and you might just get lucky this time! She might even be satisfied with the substitute for the rest of the trip (but don't count on it).

If you're going to be gone a long time, you may need to actually try to replace the favorite toy with another. You may want to tell Gina that, because this is a very special, fun family trip, you will allow her to pick out her very own special toy or stuffed animal at the next store. (You are, of course, taking a chance that the next store is one hundred miles away, and you'll have to listen to "How much longer?" for the next hour and a half.) Tell her that her forgotten special toy will be waiting for her at home, just where she left it, when she gets back.

Friends of ours avoided this situation completely by noticing very early that their daughter took comfort from a cloth diaper, which she held and used often to rub against her ear. As soon as they realized how important the diaper was to her, they set aside several of them for future use. They also substituted them often, so their daughter was actually using several different diapers. This way, the diapers all lost that new feel and smell, so that when one got lost, her parents simply

> **L**eaving a favorite toy or blanket behind can be very upsetting for a toddler. Try to be sympathetic and creative in helping to solve the problem.

substituted another from the stack the toddler had been using all along. This method works well, because if a favorite toy or blanket suddenly gets lost or left behind and parents try to substitute a brand new one, your toddler could recognize immediately, by smell and feel, that it's not the same one and may just reject it.

Jane, at eighteen months, had a special toy she called "Fuffy." Her parents had been through this with their older child, Julia, and decided to make sure there were several of the same toy around at the same time. They bought two more of them, and whenever Jane asked for Fuffy, any one of them would do. Preventing problems in the first place is always easier than having to solve them—especially at the toddler stage.

Mood Swings

At this stage, toddlers are realizing that they are a unique and separate person from others around them and that they can do some things on their own. The trouble is, they don't have the experience or ability to decide which things they can handle and which they cannot. Toddlers are also known for making a firm decision one second and changing it the next. This can result in a giggling, happy, cooperative toddler turning into a screaming, hysterical, miserable child in the blink of an eye!

> Frequent and unexplained changes in mood are very common during the toddler stage. At this age, toddlers are trying out lots of new ideas and even a new identity.

Watching these amazing changes can create lots of frustration for parents. It can be especially trying when everything seems to be going so well, and suddenly, your daughter, Sara, throws a tantrum. There are two things you can do: the first is to try to quietly calm her down. If you are already in a private place, this may mean putting Sara on your lap, rocking gently, and talking softly until she calms down.

If this doesn't work, taking Sara to a different room or even outside may distract her enough to quiet her. If she refuses to follow you, pick her up and carry her out. Looking at a book or playing with a different toy sometimes works. If you're in a public place, quieting Sara may mean taking her to a place where you can talk in private. Neither one of you needs an audience right now. After Sara is quiet, you need to talk, using words she will understand, about what just happened and what to do the next time she's feeling this way. (More tips will be covered later in the tantrums section of this book.)

> **H**olding a toddler firmly but gently on your lap can help her feel more secure.

One such example is when toddlers want to try to do something they've never done before. Kids get excited when they're allowed to try new things. They're happy and enthusiastic as they first try it out. At this age, they are often unable to finish what they start and their mood soon turns sour. Toddlers generally don't have much patience—they'll try something once or twice and if they can't do it, they often get angry, sometimes pushing, throwing, or kicking to express that anger. Since you know how it feels to be frustrated with something you can't accomplish, *try to understand what your little one is feeling*. Identifying with their frustration helps parents to be more understanding while they help their toddlers learn patience themselves.

> **T**ry to anticipate which kinds of situations cause your toddler to erupt. Some are fairly predictable, such as children finding themselves in situations that make them frustrated or embarrassed.

There are zillions of things that toddlers can't yet do at this age, and a few things that they can do very well. Concentrate on the things they *can* do: dressing themselves, eating by themselves, helping to pick up their toys or pull weeds in the garden. Red alert! Don't just send them ahead of you into the flower garden and tell them to pull the weeds—before they bloom, many flowers look a lot like weeds. I made the mistake of sending my toddler into the garden ahead of me to pull weeds. By the time I caught up with him, my three-year-old already had a pile of "weeds." You guessed it—that year, our "flower" garden turned out to be a weed garden, with about three lucky little flowers that survived our little helper!

> **S**ince mood swings can happen frequently during this age, parents need to be aware of this and steer toddlers into activities in which they have a better chance of succeeding.

Kids love to help around the house at this age (take advantage of it now—it may not last long). It makes them feel good when they do something well and you praise them for it. Of course, let them try new things, like washing the plastic dishes or putting a clean towel away, but try to keep it simple at this age. Your toddlers will be happier and their mood swings will be less frequent if you encourage them to try things that they can handle.

Most changes are hard for toddlers. Stopping one thing and starting another can be a difficult adjustment. And "time" is not a word they understand unless it means "now." Minutes can be like hours and tomorrow might as well be months away. Try to avoid some mood swings by telling your child ahead of time about changes you need to make. Explain what's coming, step-by-step: "First, we'll eat lunch. Then we'll wash up. Then we'll go to the park." It's important for you to know your own child's needs in this area. Some toddlers need a lot of warning ahead of time and some get too excited if they are told too far ahead of time. "Can we go to the park now? Is it time yet? When do we leave for the park? Is it *now*?" Just experiment with how much preparation time your own child needs and you'll figure out what works—most of the time.

Remember that all children do need some information about what's coming next so they can be ready for it. For example, Silas is playing with toys spread all over the floor and you want him to pick them up so you can both get outside for some exercise. Use a timer to show him that in fifteen minutes, when the timer rings, he will have to pick up his toys and you'll go for a walk together. Or, when it's time for Silas's nap and he says he's not tired, put him down, set the timer for an hour, and tell him that when the timer rings, he can get up. Usually, watching the timer and hearing the tick-tock will be enough to lull tired Silas to sleep and you can turn off the timer before it wakes him. If he doesn't fall asleep, however, then you have to keep your promise and let him get up when the timer rings. Letting a toddler know what's coming is an easy way for adults to reduce the number of challenges for toddlers and helps the day go more smoothly.

Whining

Speaking of challenges, we're going to discuss one right now: whining.

Whiiiiiiniiiiiiing! Whining is tough on parents. Why? Because, for some reason, whining is usually far more irritating than crying, shouting, shrieking, screaming, or even whooping, for that matter! All parents know there is a big difference between real whining and crying, talking back, or yelling.

> Toddlers often begin to whine when know they're not likely to get what they want from their parent or caregiver, are overtired, or even hungry.

Example: Mom is grocery shopping with two-year-old Leif. Mom has made sure that they shopped after a good lunch and nap, so this trip has been quite pleasant for both of them. They finish loading up the cart and begin the wait in the checkout lane. Leif spies the candy (which is precisely why the store manager puts it there!) and reaches for it. Mom says, "Not today, Leif," and moves the cart ahead as much as possible. Leif says, "Please, Mom?" Mom says, "Not this time, honey." Leif scowls, "Pleeeeze, Mom, pleeeeze?" And on . . . and on . . . You get the picture. It's sort of an unending plea for attention in a long, drawn out voice, and toddlers are especially equipped for keeping it up until you are gritting your teeth and madly counting to fifty under your breath!

Toddlers can be very determined little creatures. They're very good at trying different things to get what they want. Unfortunately, whining comes as naturally as breathing for a toddler.

As will be discussed in the tantrums section, if you give in when your children whine, they will learn

From the very first time your child whines, do not give her what she's asking for. Be firm on this one, parents.

that it works and will continue that behavior until they get what they want. It's critical to convince your toddlers that whining and acting out won't work.

For example, when Leif whines in the grocery store, his mom says, "I will listen to you if you ask me for what you want in a normal tone of voice, but not when you whine." If he continues to whine, she ignores him. This is not always easy to do, but it should work eventually, *if* you do it *every* time.

Toddlers have memories like elephants—if you give in even once to whining, they will remember that it worked, and will keep trying.

If Leif stops whining and asks his mom in a normal tone of voice for what he wants, she needs to respond immediately, not necessarily to give him what he wants, but at least to talk with him about it. If she does this every time Leif whines, eventually he'll realize that whining gets him nowhere.

Aggression

Toddlers are not great at hiding their feelings, which is why adults usually know exactly where they stand with them. As discussed previously, a toddler's mood can change from a playful, happy child one minute to a furious, out-of-control kid the next.

For instance, Grayson's mom takes him to Colin's house to play. If Colin takes Grayson's toy away, Grayson may express his anger by biting because he hasn't learned how to use words to tell Colin that he's feeling angry. Since two-year-old Grayson is just learning how to express himself, he won't understand the first time what is wrong with biting his friend. His mom needs to step in here, to tell Grayson in no uncertain terms, "We never bite!" and then take the time to show him how to handle the situation next time. She tells Grayson to ask Colin for the toy, or to come to her if he has a problem. Young children are not great negotiators, so a parent or another adult may need to be on hand to help them through situations like this.

It's not at all uncommon for toddlers to express their feelings in a way that is naturally frowned upon by adults in this society. This behavior may include biting, hitting, pinching, pulling hair, spitting, kicking, scratching, and several other creative behaviors.

Some adults have actually bitten a child back when the child bites them. Please—never bite kids back to show them that it hurts when they bite someone else. By biting them, you only show them that when they're angry they should bite because, once again, kids copy the behavior they see. Instead, in the case above for example, Grayson's mother needs to act immediately by taking Grayson's face in her hands, looking him straight in the eye, and saying, "No biting! We do not hurt people." This way Grayson understands that his mother is angry with his behavior. By being very firm, Grayson's mom makes it clear that this type of behavior is not okay.

Biting can become a more serious problem if it's not dealt with quickly and firmly. Parents must make it very clear, by explaining in a serious tone of voice, that biting is absolutely not allowed.

Healthy relationships can handle anger and firmness. Holding your toddler's face or hands gently but firmly while you also speak firmly will help your child understand that you are serious. This may be a good time for a short time-out. Removing Grayson from his play with Colin, while explaining that it was because he bit Colin, will get Grayson's attention because he doesn't want to stop his play.

Toddlers forget very quickly and move on to something else. Try to end this learning session on a positive note: make sure you tell your children that you love them but that it's the behavior you will not allow.

> **T**ry to make your point to your child and then move on. Staying angry too long doesn't make your toddler understand the situation any better.

Also, parents, it can be embarrassing for you when your toddler hurts another child and it may make you angry.

> **T**here are some people who sometimes struggle with a short temper. If you know that holding your child's face in your hands or holding the child's hands firmly will only lead to spanking or hitting your toddler, please stop yourself from even touching your child until you are calm.

Use only a very firm voice and let your toddler know you're angry, but please don't hit your child, because you will only teach your little one that it's okay to hit when you're angry. In addition, if you are very angry, you may injure your child. Step back, take a deep breath, and calm yourself down; this is good role modeling to teach your child a calming technique.

Teaching your older toddlers (closer to three years) to recognize how they feel *before* they are about to hit or bite can help them control the anger.

Actually, this advice works well for adults as well as children. When you feel yourself getting angry, have a specific behavior ready so that you can distract yourself and reduce the anger before it takes over. Once again, it's a good way to calm yourself and good role modeling for your child.

Because your little ones simply do not have the ability to reason things out, or even to talk things through, they simply react, and that may include a sock in the jaw or a kick in the shins. As a parent, you might be shocked to see your sweet little toddler haul off and smack some other sweet little toddler, but your reaction is critical here. If you get angry and swat your child on the bottom, all you've done is given your toddler another reason to hit someone—because their mom and dad hit when they're angry, too.

When your toddler begins to realize how it feels to be angry, teach him or her a different behavior instead of hitting or biting, such as picking out a different toy to play with, or even walking out of the room for a while.

That's your first message; your second message takes longer. Now your job is to teach your toddler how to handle the situation without hitting, but still allow her to express her feelings to the other child. While toddlers need to understand that they shouldn't use violence of any kind to express their feelings, they must also be given effective ways to get their point across to the other child so that they realize that they still have some power. We also want them to begin to realize how helpful words can be, even though most of them are still learning the basics of speech.

It's very logical, really—if you don't want your children to hit anyone, don't hit them. Show by your example that hitting is not allowed.

While it's important to interrupt play immediately whenever your child is hurting someone else, it is also important to remain calm while you teach your little one how to deal with this situation.

Remaining calm, however, does not mean that you can't ever show anger. It's okay to be angry, but it's not okay to hit, hurt, or shame your child. Screaming at your child only escalates the situation and you lose your opportunity to teach the lesson you want your toddler to learn.

After you've explained to your toddler what *not* to do, you need to follow up with a lesson in how to play nicely with others. Children must be allowed to learn from their mistakes, just as adults do.

When toddlers play together, there is usually a certain length of time when they play well. At some point, however, whether it's approaching nap time or lunch time or just "I don't think I like you anymore" time, the kids may simply lose it. They won't be able to handle even being in the same room any longer. At this point, the adult in charge should recognize that it's time for both kids to take a nap, or even just separate. Sometimes, it will only take a change in activity to keep everyone happy. If you read your child's cues and understand what is reasonable to expect from your toddler, you can avoid a lot of major blowups.

> **W**hen toddlers see that you are calm and in control, they are much more likely to listen to what you have to say. If you lose your patience, it will just make your toddler more upset and then you've lost your opportunity to teach.

> **S**eparating toddlers (especially two and a half years and older) when they can't get along usually works well.

Tell them that when they can play nicely without fighting, they may play together again.

Most young children, though not all, would rather play with another child than alone, so separating them is usually effective. In fact, sometimes all a parent has to do is ask toddlers if they need to play separately and they'll stop arguing. If you are consistent, reacting the same way every time this happens, your little ones will begin to understand how it interrupts playtime. Because they don't like to stop playing, it will help to teach them how to play more cooperatively.

Remember to look for chances to compliment children (of all ages) for doing things well. This positive approach makes them feel good about themselves and works much better than teaching them only when there is a problem.

Sibling Rivalry (Arrival-ry!)

A common toddler challenge is bringing home a new baby. Many families choose to have another baby from one to several years after their first. Most people have a definite opinion on the ideal age separation. Experience shows there is a very simple answer: there isn't one. Whether you wait one, two, three, or more years between babies, bringing a new person into the house to share love, time, affection, and eventually toys is often not an easy adjustment, especially for a toddler. Because much of your toddler's time is spent figuring out how he fits into your family, whether he accepts his new role as older sibling happily or resentfully is up for grabs. If he is fairly secure about who he is and feels well loved and important, he may accept the change without much trauma. Then again, he may not. You won't be sure how smooth or rocky the road will be until you are actually on it.

It's crucial to take steps to

> **W**hen you do find your toddler playing well with another child, praise them both. Try to "catch them" being good and take the opportunity to cheer them on.

> **T**he process of adjusting to a new baby, with this particular toddler and this particular new baby, is definitely an unknown. There are many things that you can do, however, to help your child get used to the idea *before* the new sibling arrives on the scene.

prepare your toddler for this major change. Ignoring the fact that a new baby will make a big difference in their daily lives, and not taking time to prepare your little ones, will make everyone's adjustment much more challenging. Just as you like to know as much as possible about major changes that are coming so that you can be better prepared to handle them, your toddler has the same need. Once again, *think about how your child is feeling.*

The better you prepare a child for something new, the easier it is on everyone.

Some suggestions:

- **Approach the change positively.** Tell your daughter that she is going to be a big sister. Emphasize all the things she can do now that she's a big girl. Talk about her role as a big sister. Explain that when she was a baby, she needed to be fed, dressed, diapered, and needed lots of naps, but now that she's big, she can take care of many things by herself. Help her feel proud of herself. Let her know that some things will change. She'll have to be quiet sometimes, but she can take long walks with her parents and baby and show the new baby to her friends. She'll have fun playing with the new baby, especially when the baby gets older.

- **Be as honest as you can** in describing what it might be like with a new baby in the house. Explain that the baby will sleep a lot, eat a lot, and sometimes cry a lot. Tell her that all of you can help to take care of the baby and soon the baby will be awake more, smile more, and be more fun to play with.

Explain that sometimes she might have to wait her turn for something because the baby will need to eat first or to take a nap first, but that all of you will help each other and try to be patient.

Describe it, but then drop it, unless she wants to talk about it again. You want to prepare her, not scare her.

- **Bring home children's books on the subject.** There are some delightful books, such as *The New Baby* by Mercer Mayer; My New Baby and Waiting for Baby, Child's Play International and the Toddler Series by Joanna Cole. Going to the library to read and pick out books to take home is fun and a very special activity to do with your child. (Remember that every time you talk, read, sing, or play with your toddler, you help stimulate brain development, an extremely important part of developing a good learner and a happy, successful child.) Reading books on the subject of the new baby helps your toddler to realize that she is not alone—that lots of other kids have gone through the same big changes. If you are an older sibling, tell your toddler what it was like for you to have a new baby at your house. Kids love to hear parents tell stories about their own childhood.

- **Involve your toddler in the experience of pregnancy.** Explain that the baby will grow inside your body, and that Mom's tummy will grow, too. When it's possible to feel the baby kick from the outside, have your toddler feel the baby move. Treat this with great excitement. You can tell your toddler that he or she kicked and moved inside you the same way the new baby is doing now. Encourage your toddler to hug you and the baby, but don't force it. Your toddler may want to wait until he or she can actually see the baby before giving hugs. Little ones will very likely have questions. Answer them simply but honestly. For example:

Q: "How did the baby get inside you?"

A: "Every woman has a very special place inside her where a baby can grow. The baby will grow bigger and bigger until it is big enough to come out."

Q: "When will the baby come out?"

A: "When the baby is big and strong enough. We will let you know when the time gets close so you can get ready for the baby along with the rest of us."

Q: "Where will the baby come out?"

A: "There is a special place between Mom's legs that will open large enough for the baby to come out when everything is ready."

At the age of two or three, toddlers can't possibly understand the complicated story of conception. Nor should you try to explain it, since you'll likely just confuse them. They don't want, nor can they understand, more detailed and involved explanations. Be honest, but remember to keep it short and simple. When they're really ready to understand the whole story, they'll probably start asking more complicated questions... but only if you have encouraged them to ask you any questions they have.

> The key to answering a toddler's questions is to keep it simple. Always let your child's questions be your guide to how much information you provide.

After the baby is born, your toddler will probably have even more questions. When your child does ask a question, avoid saying they're too young to know, because the child really only wants to be involved. Children should not be ignored when they ask a question, because if they ask too many questions that are not answered, they will stop asking them. Parents don't want children to stop asking questions—that's how they learn. That's also how adults learn what children are thinking about and what they don't understand. Parents need to encourage their children to come to them for the answers to their questions, instead of going to others. Whenever you answer your child's question, it can be a good teachable moment that allows you to teach them the values that you want them to have.

If you take the time to allow your toddler to see, touch, and hold an infant, perhaps even help to bathe the baby or help with feeding if the baby is bottle-fed, and watch while an adult changes the baby, he will have fewer questions and probably feel less worried about the coming event. He'll see that a baby takes a lot of time, but that while the baby sleeps, he can still have some special time

> Try to answer honestly every question your toddlers ask you, using words that you know they can understand, and assure them they can always come to you with any question. The ability to communicate comfortably and honestly with your teenager about sexuality or any other topic begins with comfortable, honest conversations when that same child is a toddler.

with you alone. He'll also see that babies are cute and can be fun!

- **Try to take your little one to the hospital for a visit before the baby is born,** so that he can be involved as much as possible in the plans. This way, he'll know where you're going when you leave to have the baby, and where he'll go to visit you and the new baby after the birth.

This means that your toddlers may temporarily forget the big kid things you have worked so long and hard to teach them. These may include waking up at night, toilet-training problems, or wanting more attention than usual—like

> During the pregnancy, try to arrange visits with friends or relatives who have new babies, because your child will probably be wondering what it will be like to live with a new baby.

being rocked and carried around. They may show an interest in breast-feeding or in drinking out of a bottle. They may get fussier about things in general and just need to be closer to you. If you tell them they shouldn't be doing these things, or punish them for expressing fear or nervousness about what is happening, you could make the situation worse. Once again, *try to put yourself in your toddler's shoes*, and think about the many questions that you would have about something you've never experienced before. Try to be as patient and understanding as possible to encourage your little ones to talk about how they're feeling.

> **Y**ou'll need to prepare yourself for possible behavioral changes in your toddler as your little one adjusts to this major change. Many children regress before, during, or after the new baby is born.

Try to remember that this behavior is an expression of fear and doubt and that it is just temporary! Generally, the more positively you handle this behavior, the sooner it will disappear. These are normal toddler responses to major change.

> **E**xplain that there's plenty of love in your family for both your toddler and the baby.

Or, better yet, try to set aside a special time, like after dinner every evening, as your own special time to be together—without the baby. Even ten or fifteen minutes can make a big difference. Spend special time with your older children so that they get one-on-one attention from both parents or from other caring adults. It doesn't have to be expensive to be a special time . . . it can be absolutely free!

Going into your toddler's room to spend time—just the two of you—works well. Curl up and read a book together, play a game, or just cuddle and talk. Letting your children know that you love them and want to spend time with them alone is a wonderful message for children of any age. Try to make time for these special dates because your toddler will probably feel a little left out with the new baby getting most of the attention. It doesn't always have to be a parent who takes your little one on a special outing—grandparents, aunts and uncles, and family friends can help, too. Since friends in a similar age group often have babies around the same time, trusted family friends with new babies can simply arrange to step in for each other to make each family's adjustment easier.

> **A**fter the new baby arrives, do your best to give your little ones the attention they need to help them through this adjustment period. Take your child out on special "dates," just one-on-one.

After the baby arrives, you'll also need to carefully watch your toddlers whenever they are with the new baby. Some toddlers may take out their feelings on the baby and may even try to hurt the baby. Even though this behavior may be alarming, it's a simple expression of the new feelings your toddler is having. This child has not suddenly turned into an evil monster! For example, when two-and-a-half-year-old Karen's parents brought home her new baby sister, they soon noticed that when Karen started to pat the baby, the patting got harder and harder while Karen tried to keep what looked like a very fake smile on her face! They also found Karen pinching or hitting the baby when she thought no one was watching.

Remember that these are common and normal reactions for a toddler, but you will need to react immediately whenever you see your toddler try to hurt the infant. Karen's parents sat down with her and explained that she should never hurt the baby. They said if Karen was feeling sad or angry, she should come to them to talk about it. When they had answered all of Karen's questions, they scooped her up and gave her lots of hugs and

> **T**aking a walk to the park, a ride around the lake, a trip to the library or to visit relatives or friends can make your child feel very important and well loved.

cuddling so that she knew they were not upset with her. Then, they kept a very close eye on Karen whenever she was with her new baby sister!

Your child might act out (misbehave) more often or be completely uncooperative. Watch for these cues and help your toddler express these feelings by talking to you about them. If your little one is too young to use words, make sure you give lots of extra hugs to your toddler to help reduce insecure feelings and then watch carefully whenever your little one is with the baby. Let toddlers know they are every bit as important to you as the new baby and that you understand how they feel, so that they are comfortable talking to you and expressing these new feelings.

> **A** toddler's anger may be directed at the parent, the baby, or someone else.

One very important thing to avoid, if possible, during this time is making other major changes in your child's life. For example, many parents need to make changes in the bed situation when they are preparing for the arrival of the new baby.

> **D**on't expect your daughter to move into a "big girl bed" at the same time the new baby arrives. Instead, if at all possible, make the change a few months before the baby comes—too many changes at once can be a disaster for everyone!

Tell your daughter she's going to get to move to a big girl bed because she is now a big girl (not because the baby needs the crib!). You want her to feel proud of herself and that she is being rewarded because she's a big girl now. You don't want her to see the move as being shoved out of her beloved crib because the new baby needs to take her place!

When Benjamin was three years old, his grandparents came to spend a few days while his parents went to the hospital to have his new baby brother. Ben's grandparents spent lots of time with him, playing at the park, eating ice cream, baking cookies, and reading books in the big rocking chair. Ben loved all the attention and didn't want it to stop. The day before Ben's mom and dad were to bring the baby home, his grandparents took him to the hospital to see his new brother, Seth. Ben watched as everyone took turns holding the baby; his grandparents got so involved with the baby that they paid no attention to Ben for a few minutes. Ben was then asked if he wanted to hold Seth, and he said, "No!"

After returning home with his grandparents, Ben went upstairs and was gone for about ten minutes. When his grandmother went upstairs to check on him, he wasn't in his room. She found him in the baby's room, putting the finishing touches on a mountain of toys, books, baby clothes, and diapers that he had piled inside the new baby's crib. When his grandmother asked what he was doing, he said, "Baby can't come home now—no place to sleep!"

Ben had dropped a big hint of what was to come. His parents and grandparents learned very early that they needed to make Ben feel special, too. His jealousy lasted only a few weeks, as Ben's parents made sure Ben had fun things to do and made special time for him without the baby.

Another subject that sometimes comes up is what to do during breast-feeding, if your toddler asks to have some, too. There is a natural curiosity about what breast milk tastes like and a need for your toddler to be close to you, just like the new baby. Try to think about it before your new baby comes, so you have an answer ready if it happens. You need to do what is comfortable for you.

Mia, age three, was watching closely as her mom breast-fed her new baby brother, Chang. Suddenly, she said, "Can I taste some, Mommy?" Since Mia's mom had been warned that this might happen, she had an answer ready. She explained that when Mia was a baby, she drank Mom's milk the same way, and because Chang was a new baby, he needed Mom's milk the same as Mia had when she was a baby. Mia's mom added, "But now that you're such a big girl, you get to drink milk out of a milk carton." Mia beamed. "Chang is just a baby, but I'm a big girl," and she ran off to play with her toys. This works for some toddlers, not all. Some moms decide to satisfy the toddler's curiosity by allowing their child to taste the breast milk. Often, one taste is all it takes. What the child really wants is to be rocked and held closely by Mom, just like the new baby.

Three-year-old Molly asked her mom if she could taste her breast milk. When she got close to the breast and realized it was warm, she pulled away and said, "We need to let it cool off first!" and never asked to try it again.

In summary, the better you can prepare your little one for the arrival of a new baby, the better your chances are for a smoother adjustment . . . not necessarily easy, but less stressful.

> **B**asically, what toddlers are saying when asking to try breast milk is "I want some attention, too." It's not necessarily the milk they want, but the closeness.

Tantrums

Tantrum: a word that strikes fear in the heart of every parent! A word that brings to mind a scene in the grocery store, where your sweet little daughter, Becky, has been sitting quietly in the grocery cart while you shop. She's been munching happily on the Cheerios you brought along to keep her tummy satisfied until you get home. As you wheel around the corner of aisle number seven, you realize, too late, that this is the aisle you were going to avoid. Suddenly, Becky spots the candy shelves. Whirling the cart around, you head in the opposite direction, trying desperately to distract her with more Cheerios. She completely ignores you, her once rather quiet request for candy now becoming louder and louder. Within five seconds, your cute, charming little toddler has turned into a kicking, screaming tyrant, demanding the candy, not taking no for an answer. The two of you have now become the center of attention, with everyone in sight staring at your darling little mass of misery.

Now, tantrums are not just whining, fussing, crying, or complaining. There is a very big difference between these routine toddler behaviors and a real, full-blown tantrum. For example, you and your son, Shawn, are at the park. Shawn is playing on the swings when he sees another child with an ice cream cone. He says he wants one, too. You explain that if he wants a treat he'll have to wait until he goes home and has lunch first. Shawn is not happy with this suggestion and begins to nag at you to buy him ice cream *right now*. Soon he's whining and crying, still pleading with you for ice cream. You tell him he has two choices: to leave the park and go home for lunch and a treat, or to stay and play at the park and wait until later for his treat. He finally chooses the first option and you leave for home.

This whining and crying, though irritating and sometimes embarrassing for a parent or caregiver, is definitely *not* a tantrum. It is typical behavior for a toddler to try to get what he wants. If you give Shawn a choice and explain that unless he stops whining and crying you won't listen to what he wants, he may stop. If you can see that Shawn is getting more and more upset, you may be able to avoid a tantrum by looking him right in the eye, telling him to listen to you, and giving him a choice to make. This way, both parent and child compromise—you determine the options and Shawn makes the choice.

> **A** tantrum means the child is temporarily unable to think clearly, to express needs quietly, or to calm down without help. Tantrums may include kicking, screaming, throwing things, thrashing around on the floor, and crying or yelling loudly.

Giving children a choice distracts them for a moment and also makes them feel as if they have some power in deciding what to do. On the other hand, if they continue the behavior and throw themselves on the ground, kicking and screaming, or begin to pick things up and throw them, this is no longer just fussing. It has become a full-blown tantrum.

Parents can either take immediate action or temporarily ignore their child (depending upon the setting and their own decision) to help their little one gain control once again.

> One way to handle a tantrum is to ignore it.

This usually works better when you're at home and not in church or temple, for example, during the service, where clearly other people would be affected. But let's be realistic! Have you ever met a parent whose child has never had a tantrum in front of strangers? The answer is very likely no. So encourage your relatives and friends not to be too hard on parents whose toddlers misbehave and embarrass them in public. Ask them to think back to how awful they felt when it happened to them.

Back to ignoring tantrums. Let's say Jane wants to watch TV for the third time that day. You explain that she has had enough TV and say no. Jane throws herself on the floor, kicking and screaming. As long as you know that the toddler is in a safe place where she can't get hurt, you can either go into the next room or go back to whatever you were doing. You'll need to stay close enough to keep an eye on Jane when she's not looking.

> If a toddler throws a tantrum, it doesn't mean he or she has horrible parents. It just means the child is frustrated and angry and has chosen a bad time and place to let everybody know it!

As soon as Jane no longer has an audience for her tantrum, and she's not getting her way, she may decide to stop. If she continues the tantrum, just peek at her every so often to make sure she's okay, but try not to let her see you. If she sees you looking at her, the tantrum could get worse.

When she does finally stop, praise her for calming herself down. Give positive attention for positive behavior. In this case, at home, you were able to give no attention for negative behavior.

One way to try to avoid the tantrum scene like the one with Becky in the grocery store, is to set down the rules with your child before you even enter the store.

Take a moment to tell her that she cannot buy a treat today, that she can have one as soon as you get home. Giving a toddler something to look forward to later may make it easier for the child to accept no for an answer. And it doesn't have to be food— you can say you'll stop at the playground on your way home or go for a walk, or whatever your child enjoys doing.

> **A** tantrum with no audience will often stop quickly—usually tantrums are thrown just to get attention or to try to change the parent's mind. Remember, *no audience, no performance!*

> **T**elling her *before* you even enter the store what will or will not be okay in the store is the best bet to avoid a tantrum.

Or tell your toddler she can have *one* treat at the store. You need to decide what choices she has before you enter the store, so that she's prepared for them.

Try to remember, however, there is never a guarantee with a toddler that anything you do will work. You'll just need to be prepared for anything!

Okay, let's say we have a rip-roaring tantrum in the grocery store. What's a parent to do? Here are some suggestions:

- **Take a deep breath and try to stay calm.** If you, the parent, lose control, you have probably lost the opportunity to teach.

  Head for the nearest private spot where you can deal with your child without an audience. The public restroom is usually a good place. A change in location can distract the child because he or she is wondering where you're going, and a private spot where you can talk to your child alone is *very important* at this point. Sometimes this is not possible. (A good friend tells of witnessing a tantrum in a plane during a long wait for takeoff, where there was no way to move at all. Trapped! All a parent can do at a time like this is try everything they can think of, from holding your toddler snugly but gently and rocking, to distracting the child with anything in sight. This is where cereal, crackers, small toys, or books can be a welcome distraction.) If the restroom is not available, push your cart to a far corner of the store. Among the boxes of bananas and broccoli, you may have some privacy to wait out the end of the storm. If no private spot is available, leave your cart and take your child outside or to your car. This has happened before in the grocery store. Your cart will most likely be in the same spot waiting for you when you return with a calmer child.

> **The most important goal here is not to give your child whatever caused the tantrum in the first place. If you do, you're sending the message that whenever your toddler wants something, throwing a tantrum is the way to get it.**

It is critical to deal with the behavior immediately. If you allow your child to continue screaming while you finish your shopping, you will have given the wrong message. Your child will think it's acceptable to behave like this because you didn't take action while you were in the store. Take this opportunity to teach your child what is and what is not acceptable behavior.

Usually, your child will have calmed down a bit by the time you've carried her to a private place to talk. Or she may still be kicking, screaming, or sobbing. If this is the case, she'll need your help to calm down.

Set limits by telling your child she needs to calm down so you can talk quietly about what just happened. She needs to know that you love her and that you will be there for her to make things better. Your toddler needs to feel that you are in control of the situation.

Try putting her on your lap, facing away from you. Put your arms around her and talk quietly. Tell her that when she can't calm herself down, that you will be in control for her until she can calm down. Hold her gently but firmly so that she is physically under control—this should help her feel more secure. Continue to talk softly to her, encouraging her to calm down and relax. When she finally quiets down, turn her to face you and praise her for getting herself under control again. This is a positive message to the child: you are rewarding her for behaving calmly and quietly, not for throwing the tantrum.

> **I**t's a very scary feeling for toddlers to be out of control, because they don't know how far they will go with this behavior. The parent must be the one to take control.

> **T**elling your daughter that you love her makes her realize that, even though she has made a mistake, your love is still there for her. It's crucial that you never withdraw your love for any reason.

Next, explain the rules to your toddler. Tell her that you love her, but that it is not okay for her to behave like that. Here you are separating the behavior from the child herself.

Let her know that she can learn the right way to behave and that it's your job to teach her.

Now that both of you are calmer, explain to her why having a tantrum is not the way to ask for something. Tell her that she will never get what she wants from you if she kicks and screams, but she may if she uses her words—not always, but sometimes.

Since every child is different, you will have to decide how much your toddler can understand. Keep to the point and try to explain, using words they can understand. For example, "When you want something, you must ask nicely for it. But if you cry and kick, instead of using your words, I will say no." Finish by telling her you love her and return to your shopping to try again.

> **T**aking the time to teach toddlers the proper behavior at the moment they misbehave is critical to help them understand what is proper and what is not.

Please don't say, "Wait until your father (or mother, grandmother, or aunt, etc.) comes home." By then it's too late. Toddlers won't remember what they're being punished for and you'll only confuse them. Deal with the problem immediately so they can understand how they should have acted. This way, they're more likely to remember it the next time.

Your toddler may have another tantrum about the same thing. Little ones won't learn to ride a bike the first time, or to button their jackets after one lesson, so why should they learn to pass up the candy aisle when you say no the first time? Try not to expect more of toddlers than they can give

> **S**peaking of next time, be prepared—there *will* be a next time. Learning for everyone takes time, and for toddlers, who are not able to understand why, it takes even longer.

you. Hang in there, "teacher," and they will eventually learn the lesson!

Until toddlers are taught differently, tantrums are a very common way for them to try to get what they want. If you make the message clear from the very first tantrum that this behavior will not get your toddlers what they want, but that asking for something by using words, especially "please," might work, the tantrums will more likely be fewer and farther between.

Remember, also, that your toddler is just learning to put words together. When they can't find the right words to get what they want, they naturally become very frustrated. Try to help them find the words they need to avoid the tantrum.

Tantrums also happen because parents have just said no to their child. It's very important to teach children that sometimes they will get what they want and sometimes they won't. This is a lesson that needs to be repeated often. You set the ground rules here, parents. Try very hard to stick to them when the temptation to give in gets tough. Toddlers need you to set the limits. You will both win in the end!

> **I**t is our job as parents and caregivers to try to prevent tantrums by avoiding places and situations that ask too much of a toddler.

For example, if your son has missed his morning nap or it's close to lunchtime, it's not the best time to take him shopping. He would have to sit in a shopping cart or stay right next to you in the store while your attention is on something or someone else. That's hard enough for a toddler to do even when he's not tired and hungry, but impossible to do when he hasn't had a nap or lunch. It's not fair to put your child in that position. If you must shop with your child, try to wait until after lunch or naptime.

Even better, try to get someone to take care of your little one while you shop. It doesn't even have to cost money—trade babysitting hours with another parent who may also need time away from home. This will avoid a perfect tantrum situation and both parents and toddler will be much happier. It always pays off to plan ahead to avoid an unnecessary blowup!

A common toddler behavior while throwing a tantrum is breath-holding. A child might take a deep breath and hold it—sometimes even until they pass out. It's a very scary thing for a parent to watch, but it is usually over quickly and doesn't really hurt the child. Once again, deal with breath-holding the same way you would deal with a full-blown tantrum, so the message to the toddler is that it will not work to get their way if they hold their breath. They should soon learn that it doesn't work and will try something else to get what they want. If this behavior continues, however, call your health care provider for advice.

> The minimum daily requirement for every child is at least one hug and one "I love you!" Children need to be told that they're loved often, just like adults do. Think about how much you love being loved— so does your child!

Creating and sharing a loving relationship will bring joy into your life and your child's life. When you have a good day with your child, take time to feel good about it and to experience the joy of parenting! Yes, even through the tantrum stage. Remember: this too shall pass!

Small Muscle Skills

Toddlerhood is an age of countless major changes. One of these is learning how to use those wonderful parts of the body called hands and fingers. Toddlers soon realize that fingers are not just for sucking, or for putting interesting things into their mouths, such as dandelions or Duplos or dirt. When Dad puts a piece of paper in front of his daughter, Claire, and a crayon in her hand, and presses the crayon against the paper . . . *voila*! Claire enters the world of art! Learning to make a mark on paper can spark a child's imagination and often leads to other expressions of art. For example, learning to make a mark with a crayon could easily lead to making a mark with Mom's lipstick or eye makeup . . . and not on paper this time. Maybe it would look good on the wall, on the new kitchen cabinet, or older sister's homework, or even the library book Mom just brought home yesterday! Even better, if Mom's lipstick looks good on a wall, maybe the couch could use a new design!

I'm sure you get the picture. Learning how to use her hands and fingers to have fun is just the beginning of Claire's experimentation into how to express and entertain herself. Part of teaching your child these things is to make it clear when and where and how these new things are to be used. But since it's so much fun to do, and it's such an exciting and new kind of play, expect toddlers to try new things with whatever it is they're learning. Try to be very patient while you teach your toddler. Getting angry with Claire for using the wall when she doesn't understand that there are better places for drawing won't teach her why she shouldn't draw on the walls. Do take the time to teach her carefully without expecting her to be perfect or to remember the first time you tell her something. Patience and repetition are basic ingredients for teaching toddlers . . . and don't forget the hugs!

> **A**n extremely important step for toddlers is learning that they are independent people from their parents.

One key piece of becoming independent is learning how to play by themselves, and not always needing someone else to play with. You can help toddlers to become more independent by teaching them activities that they can enjoy by themselves, such as:

- **Drawing or coloring** in a coloring book or on paper.
- **Finger-painting or painting with a brush.** Chocolate pudding or shaving cream on a cookie sheet can be a fun change from using paint, but they'll have to learn that some things can be eaten and some cannot! You can also provide water-soluble finger paints for the bathtub (but of course, bath time needs supervision!)
- **Looking at books** with bright, colorful pictures. Turning pages and pushing and pulling pop-ups in books.
- **Building with blocks or Legos.** Lego-type sets are often passed down from older to younger children and can frequently be found cheaply at garage sales. Toddlers younger than three should use the larger pieces that are too big to be put into a mouth and swallowed.

- **Putting puzzles together** is an excellent way to help your little ones learn to use their fingers for fine motor skills. Using fingers for small pieces, including peas or corn during dinner, helps to build coordination. Try to choose puzzles with just a few large pieces, so your toddler can learn to put easier ones together at first. Then slowly add puzzles with more pieces. Remember to help the first few times, but then encourage them to do it all by themselves. Then watch them do it and praise them! Help only when they're absolutely stuck and only after you've given them all the hints you can about what to do next.

Young children can get used to playing for very long periods by themselves if you help them get started. Instead of plunking them in front of the television set where they simply sit and watch, help them to use their own imaginations and actually create their own learning through play. Once again, we know that children learn best when they are having fun—play is the very best way to learn! Ask your toddlers what, where, and how they want to play. Then simply move a couple of pieces of furniture around and help them set it up. When it's ready, walk away and let them play by themselves. Sometimes they'll be happy to play by themselves, other times they'll want you to play with them. Either way, playtime should be fun learning time that allows them to use their imaginations to the fullest!

Our daughter Erica's favorite playtime activity was to play "school." At age two and a half, she would set up a chalkboard at one end of the room and put her stuffed animals in chairs or on the floor facing her. Then she would stack a pile of books next to her in front of her "students" and "read" to them. She would also tell them stories and draw on the chalkboard as she "taught"

> **I**t is very important for parents and caregivers to give toddlers time and space by themselves so that they can develop ways to keep themselves busy and happy without always having someone right there to entertain them.

school. Erica would do this for up to an hour or more at times, creating her own special fun and giving her parents time off!

Very young children need to be given simple things like plastic bowls, boxes, a spoon, a ball, and some yarn to play with while they're still less than a year old, so they can begin to use their imaginations early to entertain themselves for a while. Toddlers who have every one of the latest toys advertised on TV that walk, talk, dance, and tell stories are not necessarily being encouraged to develop their own stories or their own special interests.

Remember, especially for children under five, playing and figuring things out for themselves helps to stimulate brain development and creates new opportunities for learning!

When Erica was just nine months old, she taught us a valuable lesson. Being the first grandchild in the family, she received many toys and stuffed animals from doting grandparents, relatives, and friends for her first Christmas. After a few minutes of just sitting, looking at the toys around her, Erica crawled behind the Christmas tree and started playing with an empty box! Her family learned, very early, that simple things can make the best playthings, especially for little ones. Toddlers need to be encouraged to develop play on their own, allowing their own imaginations and interests to grow.

Big Muscle Skills

A common scene that makes most people smile is a parent vacuuming or sweeping, while a small child toddles behind, pushing a stick or a pretend vacuum or broom. Another example is seeing a parent, buried in that shivery white stuff we call snow, trying to shovel a path on the sidewalk, while a tiny, bundled-up-so-only-the-eyes-are-visible toddler shuffles behind, "shoveling" the snow right back onto the newly cleaned sidewalk!

These events often take place in the toddler stage because toddlers are just beginning to develop the ability to lift or carry, climb steadily, walk or run, catch and throw a ball, and follow clear, simple directions . . . sometimes! These new physical activities are called "gross motor skills" because they include large movements with arms and legs, not just small finger skills, as described in the previous section.

At this stage, you can expect your toddlers to run instead of walk, to climb up on almost anything within reach, and to be interested in just about everything, especially if it is dangerous or messy!

They like to swing from anything they can reach and they slow down long enough to fall asleep only when they can't hold their eyes open any longer. "On the go!" is a good description of the normal state of the toddler.

Since this is a great attitude for learning to help around the house, you can treat it as a fun game. Yes, it definitely takes more time to do everything when you have a toddler "helping," so try to plan for it. Toddlers love to help with things like grocery shopping or household chores, such as dusting, putting clothes in the washing machine, sweeping the floor, watering the plants (we highly recommend direct supervision here!), washing the dishes (plastic only, please!),

This is also "copycat" behavior time. Whatever parents are doing is exactly what the toddler wants to do.

and putting toys away. If you make it a game (you pick up one toy, then the toddler picks up one toy, etc., to see who picks up the last toy), then your children develop a positive attitude about helping you. If you never let them help because it takes too long or they don't do it perfectly, they won't learn these skills, and by the time you get around to needing their help, they'll probably have developed an "I can't do that" attitude, which may cause problems in the future.

One important point to remember when you ask your little ones to do a job: don't do it over again "for" them, when it isn't done perfectly.

> **I**t's important to begin at the toddler stage to allow—in fact, encourage—your little ones to help you do yard and housework.

Once again, *try to look at it from their perspective.* If they do the job you've asked them to do and they see you do it over again after they've finished, they'll no doubt feel sad or frustrated and certainly, disappointed. If you expect it to take longer, you won't be so impatient when it does. It's worth the extra time to include your little one in the chores. If you make it fun, it can help set a positive attitude toward chores for the future and make helping around the house a normal part of family life.

Since the toddler stage is prime time for large muscle development, it is also a great time to teach little ones the importance of exercise. Go for walks, ride your own bike or walk along while your child rides a tricycle, teach your toddlers to climb on the jungle gym, or to throw and catch a ball; these activities set a positive tone for getting exercise and having fun

> **C**hildren who grow up with no responsibilities for helping around the house won't know how to take care of themselves or their environment as they grow older.

at the same time. Simply saying, "Let's go get some exercise," and then allowing your toddler to choose the activity will help toddlers realize that exercise should be part of every day, if possible. Exercise keeps everyone healthier, and a good physical workout helps to keep everyone's stress level lower! By exercising along with your toddler, you're also being a good role model for healthy living.

Sexual Behavior and Masturbation

Human beings are sexual beings with different body parts. These differences need to be discussed and explained to young children in a positive, matter-of-fact, honest way. If these facts are given to toddlers in a simple, unembarrassed way, your little ones will understand that all of their body parts are equally important, and they will be far less likely to develop an embarrassed or self-conscious attitude about any part of their bodies. Unfortunately, some children have been taught that their sexual organs, or "private parts," are bad. Parts of the body are not bad; they are simply one of many body parts, created for a specific purpose. If your parents have communicated a negative attitude about sexuality, please avoid giving your child the same negative attitude. Children need to appreciate all parts of their bodies and to have a healthy attitude, based upon correct information, about themselves and others as sexual beings.

> **A**lways teach that both sexes are equal—create a positive view of both boys and girls.

It is very important that we teach appreciation of other people's bodies at the same time. For example, when Peter asks what makes a boy and what makes a girl, his parents say that a boy has a penis and a girl has a vagina or a vulva (although there are several specific body parts that make up the female sexual organs, it is easier to understand at this age if you just use either vagina or vulva). Please avoid saying that a boy has a penis and a girl doesn't!

> **I**t's very important for you to use the correct name for your child's sexual organs, "penis" and "vagina." Teaching anything but the correct name for sexual organs can be confusing for children.

Explain that each one is very special, for very important reasons.

As discussed in the curiosity section of this book, it is very important that you teach your little ones the proper name of every body part. You teach "ear," "arm," and "leg" comfortably and without hesitation.

If parents use names like "peepee" instead of penis, children may get the message that these body parts are different from the rest and that there is something uncomfortable about them. You may be passing on your own embarrassed or troubled attitude toward sexuality to your children. If children are taught that something about their bodies is "bad," this may create problems for them as they grow older. We may be able to help end that problem by discussing every body part openly, honestly, and positively.

Children who have been taught the correct names for all of their body parts matter-of-factly and without embarrassment have been given no reason to be self-conscious about their bodies. They are free to feel comfortable with their bodies and themselves, and to feel proud of who they are.

There is a good chance that by teaching your children the proper names for all of their body parts, you may also help to protect them from abuse.

Children who have had open and honest talks with a parent may be more likely to tell Mom or Dad or another trusted adult if something uncomfortable or abusive happens to them.

A child's curiosity is often expressed at this stage by wanting to see other people's (children *and* adults!) bodies, genitals included. Try not to overreact to this natural curiosity. Children don't consider this behavior wrong unless they have been told that there is something wrong about their genitals. Yes, definitely explain that there are some things that should be kept private. Try to explain calmly, without anger and without

> **C**hildren who have been taught the correct names of all parts of their bodies and who express themselves clearly are often better at telling other people how they are feeling and what is happening to them than children who don't know the correct names for their body parts.

shaming, that they do not show people, other than their parents, their genitals, nor should they ask to see the private parts of others.

It's very important to teach young children that if they are at all uncomfortable about anyone touching them, they should tell the person to stop and then tell their parent or caregiver about it immediately. Obviously, as your child gets older, their questions, and the answers, will get more complicated. The decision about how, when, and where to discuss sexuality is very personal; each family needs to decide how to handle this and all other developmental stages.

Except for parents, grandparents, caregivers, or specifically approved people helping with bathing or going to the toilet, or the doctor doing a medical exam, children need to be taught that no one else should touch their genitals.

A common concern in families is the issue of nudity around the house. This is a very personal decision that may be different for each family. There are some important things to keep in mind when deciding how you will handle it.

Obviously, when your children are babies or until they begin to take an interest in sexuality and body parts, it's usually not an issue. As they near two and a half to three years or so (it's different for different children), they will naturally begin to ask questions as they become aware of their own bodies and sexuality. It's always a good idea at this age to keep the answers simple.

Often questions will come up naturally; for example, when your daughter sees Dad coming out of the shower or bath. If Dad is comfortable talking to her about the difference in bodies, he can say, "Mom and you are both female and have the same body parts. Mine is different because I'm a male." If she has further questions, Dad should answer them as simply as he can.

Some people are not at all comfortable with nudity in the home. In that case, make sure you're covered when your child is around. However, you will still need to answer any questions your children may have so that they always feel they can come to you for answers to any questions.

Each family must do what's comfortable for them in terms of nudity. Parents may be very comfortable with nudity in the privacy of their own homes, especially when their children are very young. Some parents bathe or shower with their babies and very young children.

As children get older, however, they typically want more privacy themselves. Parents, also, might change their minds about being nude in front of their older children. It is a very personal decision for each family member.

Also explain that other families may have different ways of doing things, and that they may not be the same as yours. Even if your family is comfortable with nudity, explain

> **L**isten to your children and make sure you respect their need for privacy, just as you want them to respect yours.

to your toddler that when her little friend, Suzy, comes for an overnight, you'll all wear pajamas!

Gender Roles and Identity

Before the age of about two years, toddlers don't realize that there is any difference between the sexes. They see other people simply as people, not as female or male. As they reach the toddler stage, however, children generally become much more aware of how their bodies work and what they look like. Toddlers proudly show each other their "big muscles," stand back-to-back to see who is taller, and have races in the backyard to see who can run faster. These little ones are very curious about how they stack up against their friends, male or female.

> **T**his natural curiosity helps them to figure out who they are and what role they play within their family and within their own little circle of friends.

98

With this curiosity about how their bodies work comes a very natural curiosity about how other peoples' bodies look and work. One day your male toddler will come to the realization that he is a boy and your female child that she is a girl. This often results in the child creating a strong identity with the parent of the same gender.

Parents and caregivers, this is a red alert! Since your toddlers are so aware of the roles adults play, please make sure to provide them with a wide variety of activities that both genders are capable of doing. Moms, as well as dads, grandmas, aunts, uncles, and friends can mow the lawn, fix things around the house, cook, clean, or do the laundry and often, both parents go to work outside the home. Try to encourage your toddlers to play with toys of all kinds. Please don't stop your children from becoming all that they can be by giving them only toys that in the past have been given only to one specific gender (for example, trucks and cars for boys, dolls for girls). Most boys eventually become dads. You can give your son a positive role model to imitate if Dad or other males in his life take responsibility for childcare, cooking, cleaning, and other things around the house. The same applies for your daughter. Mom works outside the home, fixes things, mows the lawn, and puts gas in the car.

When adults take on only the jobs that have been traditionally limited to males or females, based strictly upon their gender, they may be limiting their own children in the way they look at themselves and the things they decide they can (or should) do.

Let them see, by your behavior, that both men and women can do almost anything, and that they help each other to do all the things that need to be done every day. This way, you teach not only cooperation, but you also teach them that all people are responsible for themselves, and should be strong and independent enough not to always

> **E**specially at the toddler stage, children may identify very strongly with the same-sex parent or caregiver. They will copy the behavior they see. Therefore, it is very important that parents give their little ones the message that they can do almost anything!

depend on others to do things for them. Try not to let society's past expectations limit your child's future expectations!

Most of all, help your little ones to feel they are capable of handling whatever they face, and if they need you to help, you'll be there for them. Giving the message that your daughter can't do something because she's a girl, or your son that he can't because he's a boy may be putting up a mental roadblock to the goals they set for themselves. Encourage them to be everything they can be—then get out of the way and watch them succeed!

Sometimes parents worry that their actions might change their child's sexuality. Your child's sexual orientation is set at birth, whether heterosexual, homosexual, or bisexual. Your child is who he or she is at birth.

> **Y**our job as parents is to accept who your children are and to help them become healthy, secure, self-confident children who can enter into loving relationships as adults.

Children come as is—with a set personality, talents, likes, dislikes, and all kinds of other things that show up gradually as the child grows older. Allowing your daughter to help glue a broken chair or play sports or your son to help bake cookies or sew on a button will not change them into something they are not. Exposing them to different situations and teaching them as many skills as possible will make them stronger, more confident, and more independent adults.

If you come upon your toddlers with their clothes off, playing "doctor" with another child, try not to overreact! Toddlers are naturally curious—they compare body parts just as innocently as they compare color of eyes or hair. Simply tell them to put their clothes back on and play something else. After they're dressed, you might do one of two things: either explain to both of them that certain things are to be kept private, and explain what those things are or, if you're not comfortable talking to the other child about the issue, take your own child aside later and talk about it. Make sure you ask if they have any questions and answer them simply but fully. Please don't punish your little one for doing what comes naturally for a toddler.

There is room for concern, however, if the play involves children of large age differences, if force is used by one child against another, or if any sexual acts are involved. There may be two concerns here: if this happens, you will need to know what behavior the other child is mimicking—he or she may be a victim of sexual abuse. The other issue is the impact on your own child. Please get immediate professional help if your child is ever the victim of this type of sexual activity. Children who receive help quickly usually respond much better than children who wait months or even years for help.

Masturbation is another subject that many parents and caregivers find disturbing. Some people either react completely negatively, even angrily, or they may even laugh at or humiliate the child in front of others. Either of these reactions may be damaging to a child. Toddlers explore their world in order to find out how things work, how they feel, what to do, and what part they play in this big world.

One of the first things that babies explore is their own body.

As infants, they suck on their fingers and toes, pull at their ears, poke at their belly buttons, smear food through their hair, and stuff everything they can into their mouths to see how it tastes and feels. As adults, we cheer them on when we see them do these things (except, maybe the food-in-the-hair part!). We know they are discovering how different parts of their bodies work, which is important for them to do. Why, then, are we embarrassed when our male toddler's hands explore his penis? It's just another part of his body, easy to hold on to, changing in shape and size, and it feels good, too. It's a natural step in his development to figure out how *all* parts of his body work.

Sometimes a little boy holds his penis for security, completely unaware that he is even holding it. Sometimes he has to go to the bathroom! Sometimes you'll see a little girl rocking back and forth on the arm of a chair, or even while sitting on a large stuffed animal. She has discovered that when she does this, it feels good. Sometimes a male toddler will walk around with his hands down his diaper or pants. Sometimes a female toddler will be sitting and watching TV with her hands between her legs, totally unaware of what she's doing.

These children are simply expressing their human sexuality—it is as much a part of them as their brown eyes or curly hair.

Your job, as parent, is to realize that this is a very natural part of human development—and to treat the whole incident as calmly as possible. Any kind of punishment for simply doing what comes naturally will make no sense to your child. This simply draws their attention to it and may send the message that there is something different or bad about their sexual organs.

When Joey was three years old, his grandmother was visiting at his house. Joey, with his hands down the front of his pants, came into the living room where his mother was talking with his grandmother. Grandma was shocked and raised her voice, saying, "Joey, stop that! You should never . . ." That was when Joey's mom interrupted her to say, "Joey, if you need privacy, please go into your room and close the door." Joey turned and went directly to his bedroom. While he was gone, Joey's

When you see your little one masturbating, you could ignore it, because it is normal, or you could distract the child by suggesting another activity. This, of course, depends upon whether you are in a public or private setting and your own decision about that. Distraction works well. This way, you don't draw attention to the behavior, and the child simply does something else.

mom explained to his grandmother that she believed that Joey was simply doing what was natural for a toddler, exploring his body. Fortunately, Joey's grandmother was willing to try to understand why Joey's mom chose to treat the matter with a very calm and matter-of-fact attitude, rather than to react with shock and punishment. Joey, meanwhile, was out of his room in less than thirty seconds, playing happily with his dump truck. By explaining to Joey that he should go into his room because this is something that is only done in private gives him the choice to either stop what he's doing and stay to play, or go into his room alone. Usually toddlers don't want to be separated from the group, so they'll stop in order to stay with everyone else.

Every family needs to teach their children their own values and handle each situation based upon those values. As a toddler explores his or her own body, it's natural for them to touch themselves everywhere. A calm and matter-of-fact reaction by parents helps to keep the behavior in perspective as a normal toddler developmental issue.

> It's important to allow children to accept their sexuality as a natural part of who they are and for parents to accept it, as well.

CHAPTER 5

Sleep Issues

How did you sleep last night? Did you fall asleep right away? Did you toss and turn because you were worried about something? Did you lie awake for a while before you fell asleep, thinking about something that had happened that day . . . or about something you had to do the next day? Or did you fall asleep from exhaustion as soon as your head hit the pillow?

We're talking, of course, about sleep problems. There are many different kinds of sleep problems, especially at the toddler stage.

Trouble Falling Asleep

As you know, falling asleep isn't always easy for adults, and children are no different. We, as parents, sometimes don't understand why our little ones don't just fall asleep when it's bedtime because all they've done is play all day and they certainly don't have anything to worry about that would keep them awake. After all, you pay the bills, cook the meals, make sure your children are loved and safe from harm. What else could they possibly have to worry about?

Surprise! They have plenty to worry about! Why? Because they're toddlers! This stage of childhood is full of real and imaginary fears that tend to keep a child awake at night. These fears can also create bad dreams. Let's

> **W**hen it's time to go to sleep, they often worry about being separated from those they need and love.

talk about the reasons why your little one may not have an easy time sleeping.

Going to sleep is a very big deal for a toddler. During the day, your little ones have been learning how to do things for themselves, and feeling more and more confident about not needing an adult to do things for them every time. But there are still many things that they cannot do alone, and they begin to realize that they really need someone to help many times during the day.

They go from a light, awake world, where they have some control, to a dark, asleep world, where there is no control. Not only is the dark world often scary and mysterious for little ones, going to sleep means they have to give up playing and then be separated from the rest of the family.

They must practice this over and over, until they begin to realize that they can fall asleep, be safe during sleep, and wake up to find their loved ones right there for them.

> **L**earning to fall asleep feeling safe and secure is a very important step in a toddler's life.

Consider this scene: you've finished the regular bedtime routine and said good night, and your child keeps calling for you.

Did she have a three-hour nap? How much exercise did she have? Is she nervous or excited or frightened about some event that's happening tomorrow? Is she off schedule by an hour and a half because the whole family slept late this morning? Did she have a scary experience that day? Is she beginning to need less sleep? Many times parents can figure out why their child can't get to sleep.

> **B**efore losing your patience, put yourself in your child's shoes and ask yourself what kind of day your toddler had.

If, after going through your normal bedtime routine, your little one still can't fall asleep, try setting a timer for ten or fifteen minutes, telling your toddler that she should listen to the gentle tick-tick of the timer. Tell her to watch the arrow move and when it rings, you'll come back to check on her. Between the ticking sound and watching the arrow move very slowly, toddlers often fall asleep. Soothing music works well, too. Play her favorite lullaby softly and tell her you'll check on her when it's done playing.

When our two-year-old son was having trouble learning to go to sleep on his own, we did the following: The first night, we sat on a chair next to his bed for a few minutes, telling him to go to sleep. The next night, we moved the chair a little farther away from his bed. We continued to move the chair each night until we were actually outside his room. The last night he called for us, we told him that we were there and to go to sleep. From that night on, he realized that we were out there and went back to sleep by himself if he woke during the night. Children need to learn how to get themselves back to sleep when they wake during the night. It's a skill they'll use for the rest of their lives.

> Children who learn how to get back to sleep on their own will usually be less frightened of the dark and better sleepers eventually.

A small plastic glass of water near the bed can be the answer for a thirsty child (two and a half to three years old) at night. A night-light can reduce fear of the dark. Taking a stuffed animal to bed can help with loneliness.

Giving children a positive reason or reward for appropriate behavior often works well. Now, we aren't talking about a trip around the world for going to sleep! We are talking about having a small surprise the next morning, such as a colorful sticker or a favorite treat if, and only if, she doesn't call you into her room again and if she goes to sleep by herself. Please understand, you aren't setting up this deal for the rest of her life. This is one way parents can occasionally deal with a behavior they want to

> If they've gone to sleep by themselves, compliment them the next morning when they wake up.

change. When your child has proven to herself that she can get to sleep on her own, it usually becomes easier for her to do so. At this point, you gradually reduce the number of times you offer a reward and eventually stop it completely when she has learned the behavior.

Parents will need to be very patient and understanding until their toddlers develop the belief that going to sleep, just like many other things they do during the day, is something they can do by themselves. Try to be patient but firm. It's a gradual process, like most things at this stage.

Regular Bedtime Routine

Toddlers are not usually happy when they're faced with a lot of changes in their daily routine.

> **W**hen children can depend on a regular schedule, doing basically the same things at about the same time every day, they feel more secure.

If they don't have to deal with lots of changes during the day, that suits them just fine. The same thing holds true for the bedtime routine. If one night you put the child to bed at nine o'clock, the next night at seven, and the third night at nine thirty, the child doesn't have a chance to get into a good daytime-nighttime body clock schedule. A body clock refers to the way the body adjusts to a daily routine. Think of your own schedule. If you go to bed very late one night, you're probably tired the next day. You either want to take a nap during the day or try to get to bed early the next night. Your body very clearly tells you when it needs more sleep and when it has had enough. When you are able to go to sleep at about the same time every night, and wake up at about the same time every morning, you generally have more energy and are happier during the day.

Your children respond the same way. Try to keep them on a regular schedule. It's easier on everyone. Set a specific bedtime and stick to it. Of course, it won't be possible to keep it to the exact minute every night, but do try. When our children were toddlers, we settled on the following routine: One-half hour before bedtime, we told them that it would soon be time for bed and that after they brushed their teeth and got into their pajamas, we would read some books (short stories, not novels!) and then we would talk for a few minutes about the day. We continued to "warn" them a couple more times as bedtime got closer. One of the reasons this routine worked well for us is because *we repeated it every night.* Toddlers will usually be much more ready to go to bed if they know exactly what's coming and when, especially if they slow their activity level way down before they climb into bed.

If you give the child a bath before bed, begin the bedtime routine an hour before bedtime, because you'll still need about twenty to thirty minutes of quiet time before bed. If baths include noisy and exciting water play, they are definitely not considered quiet time!

Providing your toddlers with books is a simple and effective first step to help your child learn many things, including developing prereading skills that will prepare them for success in school and in life. Many studies have shown that children whose parents read to them are

> A great bedtime activity is reading (or telling) fun stories (definitely *not* scary stories!) to your child. Introducing your child to books as early as possible will start them happily on the road to fun and exciting learning.

> The library is a wonderful place to spend time with your child . . . free! Bring lots of books home to enjoy together and teach your toddler how to handle books gently.

generally better readers, better spellers, and have a better vocabulary. Begin reading and telling stories when your child is an infant—studies show that simply talking to your baby or toddler is an excellent way to help your child's brain develop and to develop a strong, loving bond between the two of you. Talking, singing, reading, or telling stories are very important ways that parents can help their children get ready for learning in preschool or kindergarten.

At bedtime, hold your children on your lap or tuck them into bed and sit on the edge of the bed or in a chair near the bed to stay close to them. This is a special time for you to be close and loving. If you have more than one child, separate bedtime routines can become too long; again, this is completely your choice. You may want to take all the children into the same room, or tuck them into the same bed to read books. Allow each child to choose one book, or take turns choosing one each night, so they all have one special story for themselves. (Often they will choose the same story every night. Soon, you won't need to read the book; you'll all have it memorized!) Read aloud with a quiet voice and turn down the light, if possible. You need to tell your children how many stories you will read so they can't make quiet time two hours long.

> Children like to hear stories about themselves or about their parents, way back in the dark ages when Mom and Dad were kids.

Even a fifteen-minute routine can often take extra patience, especially when both parent and child are tired. Taking this time, however, will make bedtime more pleasant for everyone.

Another quiet time activity you might choose is to tell stories to your child. Some families prefer to tell each other stories or to take turns telling parts of the same story.

Favorite bedtime activities for our family were to sing songs or recite nursery rhymes. Some parents and children make up their own rhymes and have lots of fun doing it. Whatever is fun and relaxing for you and your child is the best choice.

Bedtime can be a good end-of-the-day listening time. Try to take this special time with your children to listen to whatever they want to tell you. When your little ones are quiet and relaxed, take a few minutes to talk about anything they bring up. Sometimes they'll talk about fears or concerns that have been bothering them. It's also a good time to talk about what tomorrow's schedule will be, especially if it's different from the normal routine.

> **"I** love you" is a wonderful message for a child to hear before falling asleep.

If you take the time to listen and make this part of your nighttime routine when your child is very young, it may always be your time to talk about problems or concerns, even through their teen years. Taking this time also shows your children that you love them. That message can be given to them many different ways every day.

An especially effective part of bedtime can be singing. Now, wait a minute . . . I know what you're thinking! You're afraid if you started singing, your son would put his pillow over his head or your dog would start howling! Not true. You don't have to be an opera singer for your little one to enjoy listening to you sing. Just choose a slow, lullaby-type song

> **G**entle human touch is extremely important in creating a loving, trusting, secure child.

and sing softly. The gentle rhythm of a song can often soothe a child to sleep.

A back rub or head rub can also be very calming for a child. *Again, just think how relaxing it is when you have one.* It's fun to be creative with your back rubs. Two-year-old Katie loved to have a garden "planted" on her back, beginning with gentle hoeing and raking, followed by planting rows of seeds. Next came the warm sun and rain, followed by the

> **H**ugging and holding, an arm around the shoulder, or a pat on the back feel wonderful for both you and your child. Sometimes a hug can say "I love you" or "I'm proud of you" even better than words.

"harvest." Or, if your child is beginning to learn the alphabet or numbers, trace a letter or number on your toddler's back and have him guess what it is. Just use your imagination!

Bedtime is an especially good time for snuggling with your child. Touch is very soothing and relaxing and will help your little one fall asleep feeling well loved.

Remember, it's not possible to spoil children by hugging them too often. The opposite is true—not hugging or holding a child often enough may create a lonely, insecure child. Hug your child often, especially during stressful times, and you'll *both* be happier!

Fear of the Dark

Many toddlers go through a phase when they are afraid of the dark. Telling them there's nothing to be afraid of is not helpful. For your child, there *is* something to be afraid of. Try to remember how you felt when you were a child, dealing with fears. We want our children to understand that they are not alone in feeling these fears. We don't want them to feel there's something wrong with them for feeling scared. Just saying, "I understand how you feel . . . sometimes I was afraid of the dark when I was little, too" can be a great relief to your child. You can leave a night-light on or a small lamp somewhere in the room. Be prepared, however, when you turn on the small light,

> Leaving the hall light on or leaving the door open slightly may also work.

> Talking with and listening to your children whenever they need it tells them you love them, that they are worth your time, and that you respect them and care enough to listen to them.

111

for shadows to appear on the wall—you just may be back to dealing with the monster thing again!

Our son, Andrew, had a closet door full of glow-in-the-dark star and planet stickers, which he stuck on by himself, to help keep him company at night. These stickers are very inexpensive and can sometimes be very comforting to a child.

Eventually, your toddler will begin to understand that being afraid of the dark won't last forever. Parents need to remember this, too. This is usually just a phase; be patient and help your children to express their feelings, no matter what they are.

Phases typically won't last as long if you're helping the child to deal with it. Your toddler needs to feel trust and security in order to get over fears. A calm, understanding, "let's talk about it" attitude can make an enormous difference in helping your child through any challenging phase.

Just One More Drink of Water

Toddlers are brilliant when it comes to excuses for staying up late, and they get better at it as they get older. If you have completed your bedtime routine and you know your child is tired and needs sleep, it's time to say good night and leave. Allowing your little ones one more drink of water, one more book, one more of anything because they whine and cry will give the wrong message. As we have discussed in the tantrums section, giving in to toddlers because they whine or cry will encourage them to repeat that same behavior over and over again.

> Parents need to set rules and stick to them. Children need parents to set limits because they cannot set their own limits and it's scary to be out of control. Children learn to trust that their parents will be in control when they are not. Limits provide a sense of security for children.

Popping out of Bed

An extremely frustrating and common naptime or bedtime challenge is having your little ones get up out of bed not once, but many times after you've put them down. If it's happening at night, check the daytime schedule. It may be that they are napping too long or too late in the afternoon and aren't tired by bedtime. If it's a daytime nap issue, you might try the following suggestions: be very firm, saying, "You must stay in bed. When you wake up, we'll go play outside, but you have to take a nap first." Then, pick the child up and place the toddler firmly back in bed, each time.

> The last thing you want to do at night is to reward your children by playing with them or by letting them stay up, even for a little while. You need to be consistent and firm.

When they finally realize you won't give in and play, they will often give up and go to sleep. When they do wake up, compliment them for staying in bed and then give them the reward you promised. They should eventually connect the reward with staying in bed.

If you've tried this for a couple of weeks and bedtime is not improving, you may need to try something that works better than just encouragement. Some little ones need only to hear that they are a big boy or girl to change behavior. Other children need more. A positive approach to changing this behavior is again recommended.

Choose something that your child likes as a reward: going to the park, having a picnic, having a special treat when they wake up. Small treats work wonders; a piece of fruit or a small sweet won't hurt your child or even spoil an appetite for breakfast or dinner.

> If your toddlers are able to understand the connection between doing what you want them to do and getting something for themselves in return, then small rewards usually work well.

If you would rather not use food, please choose something your kids really (*really!*) like; otherwise, they'll have no reason to change their behavior. Activities that you and your child can do together (going to the park, taking a special walk, reading extra books, having a picnic on the living room floor) are especially fun and can strengthen the bond between you and your toddler. Tell them that if they stay in bed, they will get a reward. The key here is to do what you promise—immediately or as soon as possible—because the child must be able to connect the positive behavior with a fun reward. As you continue this system and very gradually stop offering the reward, your little ones should begin to get used to the new behavior and begin, after some point, to do it on their own without the reward.

Another suggestion (this one usually works better for children two and older) is to make a chart for your toddler's bedroom wall. Draw the days of the week and use either a shiny colored sticker or just draw a star (or have your child draw it) for each day your child doesn't get out of bed. Every time you put a star on the chart, make a big deal of how proud you are of your toddler for staying in bed. When there are a certain number of stars in a row (three, four, or five) your child has earned a little reward.

> **T**ry to be flexible—if your toddlers have had a particularly long sleep the night before, don't try to force them down for an early nap.

A word about naps: the need for naps during the day varies greatly among young children. Most toddlers need a nap during the day until they are about three or four. Some sleep two hours, some only half an hour. Once again, every child is different. For example, don't expect your second child's naptime schedule to be the same as your first.

This will surely result in an argument, especially if your child isn't tired. *Once again, think about how your child is feeling.* It will help you to be more understanding and effective.

It's important to be aware of your child's need for sleep.

It's very helpful to have a regularly scheduled naptime, if at all possible. If you have not been able to give your child a nap and it's five thirty or six o'clock pm, it's generally better to forget it. Tired children often fall asleep early all by themselves. If they take a late nap, they'll probably sleep until their normal bedtime and then want to play. At that point, everyone's schedule is off.

One possible pitfall is when you allow your little ones to wear you down and you finally give in. You might let them stay up later or climb in bed with

> **M**ayo Clinic recommends twelve to fourteen hours of sleep daily for toddlers: about fourteen hours for toddlers fifteen to eighteen months, and twelve or thirteen hours for two and a half to three years.

you (again, this is your decision, depending upon the circumstances and your family's needs). However, your toddler will likely remember that and keep trying for a repeat performance. Be consistent with naptime . . . in the long run, it will pay off for both of you.

Night Waking

Another common sleep problem for toddlers is waking up during the night. There can be several reasons for this. Just remember there is a reason each time your children wake up, but often they can get back to sleep on their own, *if* you don't rush into the bedroom at the first squeak and pick up the child. There are many things you can do to teach your little ones to sleep through the night.

> **R**emember that we all have periods of light sleep during the night when we wake up briefly.

Studies show that most of us then simply repeat the way we first fell asleep. For example, if we turned on our side and snuggled the pillow under our chin to fall asleep, we'll do the same thing when we wake up briefly during the night in order to get ourselves back to sleep. This is exactly what you want to teach your little ones to do.

They need to learn how they, too, can make themselves comfortable—like they did when they fell asleep earlier—and fall back to sleep by themselves.

If your three-year-old son wakes up and comes into your room, and if he is not upset about a dream or frightened about something, simply give him a hug, then tell him it's nighttime and that he must go back

> **I**f parents rush in as soon as they hear the first little peep, their toddlers don't have the chance to learn how to get back to sleep on their own.

to bed. With some toddlers, this works. He realizes that you're not going to get out of bed and play with him, so he just returns to bed. Some toddlers are more challenging. Parents may need to get out of bed and take the child back to his room and tuck him in.

> **A**t night, remember the two Bs: *brief* and *boring*!

Any time you need to deal with your toddlers during the night, unless, of course, they're sick, make it *brief* and *boring*. You don't want to give the child the idea that this is playtime. Your little ones will learn that nothing fun happens if they wake up during the night, so they will have no reason to do so. This makes it very clear that nighttime is for sleeping, not for playing. Then make sure you provide plenty of hugs, snuggles, and playtime during the day to reassure the child and reinforce the idea that daytime is for cuddling and play. Nighttime is for sleeping.

Fair warning: it is not at all unusual for toddlers to learn to sleep on their own and then a few weeks or even months later begin waking at night again. Be patient and follow the same routine you used the first time. It should take less time each time they slip back. Remember, every child is different. Some will take less time, some will take more—just hang in there. It will be worth it for future peaceful nights!

Nightmares

Almost all young children have occasional nightmares. Just like adults, children have lots of things going through their minds, not just during the day, but at night, as well. Toddlers, especially, have fears that bother them. Those fears are often the reason for a nightmare. Usually, by the time the parent knows the child is having a nightmare, it's over. Your little one is either at your bedside crying or sitting up in bed calling out for you. They can sometimes tell you exactly what the nightmare was about. A very typical bad dream has monsters in it, or a scene where the child is falling, or where something big is chasing them. Every child is different, of course, and every dream has different villains in it.

Tell them they're safe and that it's okay to go back to sleep. Emphasize that the bad dream is all gone now. You may need to stay for a few minutes until they fall asleep. Nightmares can be very scary and seem very real. Your toddler needs to feel safe and secure to go back to sleep.

> **A**ll a child usually needs is to be hugged and comforted by you and told that it was just a dream and not real.

When a child has the same basic nightmare over and over again, you will need to talk about it during the day. If, for example, your daughter dreams that she is being chased by the neighbor's dog, you need to reassure her during the day that she is safe from that dog. You can actually go to the neighbor's yard and show her that the dog is tied up or behind the fence and that he can't get out. Or you may be able to actually make friends with the dog (only if this is a very friendly-type mutt who doesn't eat visitors for lunch!).

> **D**ealing with something that's troubling your child during the day can often prevent nightmares at night.

Some people use "worry dolls" to help their older toddlers get over fears or to help them express their feelings. These are a set of little dolls, which fit inside a tiny box. Toddlers, especially by the time they're three years old, can tell their troubles to the dolls while playing. Some children can express their feelings more easily by talking to a doll or favorite toy instead of to a real person. Always encourage your little ones to talk about feelings with you and start that open communication very early, but if you have a child who is not comfortable doing that, at least not every time, the worry dolls might help.

Another very common reason for nightmares is watching something scary or violent on television or in a movie. One of the most important responsibilities of parenting is to protect your little ones from things that can harm them. As was stated earlier, violence in real life, on TV, in movies, and in cartoons can frighten a toddler and sometimes create more serious problems. Do everything you can to prevent violence in your child's life.

Finally, and most importantly, children with lots of nightmares— every night or even several times a week—may be trying to tell you something. Try to get these little ones to talk about things that are bothering them. Also, think about your home situation or the babysitter or daycare situation. Have you changed your normal routine? Do you have a new baby in the house? Is there an older child in the neighborhood picking on your toddler? If your kids are showing signs of stress (sleeplessness, anxiety, more than the normal toddler irritability) and begin to have frequent nightmares, it is very important for you to find out what the trouble is. If you can't figure out what the problem is, and it continues, ask your doctor for help.

Sleepwalking

Sleepwalking is another example of a fairly common, usually temporary, nighttime problem. Remember that sleepwalkers are in a confused, half-awake state. Talking them out of it usually won't help. Very gently lead them back to bed. Simply tucking them back in is usually all that's needed.

As a parent, you must make sure that the bedroom is as safe as possible to walk in if your child is occasionally a sleepwalker. Have your toddler pick up everything off the floor before bedtime.

If you close the bedroom door at night, you may want to fasten some small bells to the doorknob so that you will hear the door if it is opened. If you leave the door open, you can hang a string with small bells tied to it from the doorframe, so that you can hear the child leave the room.

> **A** temporary gate may be needed at night to prevent a sleepwalker from walking or falling down the stairs.

Also, make sure your child cannot open the outside door and actually walk outside the house or apartment. Obviously, the dangers outside are much worse than inside your home. Sleepwalkers must be protected.

The Family Bed

This is a sensitive and sometimes emotional subject for some families. For many cultures around the world, and for some in America, the family bed is a normal and accepted practice. For some families, it's a practical solution, due simply to the number of beds available.

> **N**early everyone has an opinion about whether children should sleep in the same bed with their parents, either briefly or on a permanent basis.

Some people believe that children feel more secure with a parent beside them. Others feel it can be emotionally damaging for children to sleep with their parents on a long-term basis. You must decide for yourself what works for your own family.

One of our objectives as parents is to create a strong bond of love, respect, and trust between ourselves and our children. All parents want the best for their children; they want them to become loving, kind, happy, generous, independent people, who feel good about themselves and what they can accomplish. Parents want to give their children what they need in order to be able to believe in themselves and to take responsibility for themselves and the world around them.

One way to help them understand this is to provide them with their own bed to sleep in. Parents have their own bed to sleep in, too. We are definitely not saying that climbing into bed during a scary thunderstorm or following a scary experience or nightmare is a bad idea. Jumping into bed with parents in the morning is warm and snugly and fun! Allowing them to go to sleep in your bed instead of their own, however, may or may not create problems later on and once again, it is each family's decision to make.

> **W**hen you're deciding how to handle this issue, consider how important it is for toddlers to learn that they are separate people from their parents.

Before you decide to allow your children to sleep in your bed instead of their own, you might want to know what you're getting into. We all know that both adults and children need a good night's sleep. Having a toddler's feet in your face or getting kicked every ten minutes generally does not make for a restful, deep sleep. If you wake up tired because of this, chances are you may not have the patience it takes to deal with a toddler the next day.

> **T**ired kids plus tired parents can be a challenging combination.

Another thing to consider is privacy. Adults may want the freedom to decide to have sexual relations without having a child observer. Assuming your kids won't wake up if you decide to make love while they sleep in the same bed is definitely wishful thinking. Children who do wake up to see parents making love can sometimes become confused about their own role in this situation.

It can also be a mistake to assume that after your children are used to sleeping with you, it will be fairly easy to get them to start sleeping in their own bed when you decide it's time for a change. Toddlers are more comfortable with the same routine. Major changes like this one can be very challenging to deal with. This is especially true if your little one must also face other changes at the same time, such as adjusting to a new brother or sister or sharing a formerly single parent with a new partner. Getting moved from the comfort of your bed while also having to share a parent with someone new can create challenging problems for your child and for the entire family.

Independence is an important part of growing up. When toddlers learn to sleep safely and unafraid in their own beds, it gives them a daily message that they can be separate and independent from others in their world.

> **O**ne of the best reasons to give your children their own sleeping space is to create and encourage a sense of independence.

Clearly, this issue is an important one, since the decision you make for your child as an infant can affect your own sleeping pattern for years to come. But please remember that if you do try it, and then decide it's not right for your family, you'll need to consider *gradually* transferring your child to a separate bed.

Two-year-old Michael began getting out of his own bed at night and going into his parents' bed to sleep. After a few weeks of being awakened by Michael in the middle of the night, his parents finally gave in and decided to try the family bed. Michael liked it, but his parents missed their privacy, and as Michael got older and bigger, his movement in the bed kept them from getting enough sleep. When Michael turned three, his parents decided to switch him back to his own bed, but knew they would have to do it slowly to make it easier on their son.

They started by creating what they told Michael was "a very special bed just for Michael" on the floor of their bedroom. Michael liked his new bed and adjusted to it well. Michael's parents kept telling him how he was a big boy now, and how big boys got to sleep in their own beds. After a few days, Michael's parents helped Michael fix up his own "big boy" room, with his own special artwork on the walls, and a fun play area in one corner with his favorite books and toys, so that he enjoyed being in there. A few nights later, they moved Michael back into his own room, and put him to bed with his favorite stuffed animal after quiet time.

Michael complained the first few nights, saying he didn't want to sleep alone. So Michael's parents would lie down with him for a few minutes before he fell asleep. They gradually shortened the time they stayed with him, and soon he fell asleep on his own. A couple of nights Michael got up and tried to get into his parents' bed, but his mom told him that he had his own special sleeping place now, and that if he left his bed, she would take him back every time. Michael soon realized that getting up wouldn't work, and soon he was going to sleep in his own bed and sleeping through the night.

This process took a lot of patience and several weeks, but Michael's parents respected their son's feelings enough to make this big change slowly. Therefore, Michael had no major problems adjusting. An abrupt change in routine for most children can create problems.

> **M**aking changes gradually is very important for toddlers, especially with something as important as sleeping arrangements.

The family bed decision is an important one. Some parents feel that the family benefits from sleeping in the same bed. This is not a new idea—it is done in many cultures around the world. As you decide what's right for your family, you may want to consider the scenarios described above to determine if it will work for you.

A different philosophy is that if everyone understands from the beginning that they each have their own bed, and plenty of love and hugs are given during the day, it will help create happy, secure children who never expect to sleep anywhere but their own beds. It is also important to remember, however, that every family needs to decide for themselves what will work best for their own particular situation.

SUMMARY

How does one sum up the toddler? One-word descriptions are hard to come by for this age group. The closest I can come with any accuracy is "unpredictable."

We know that it is critically important for parents to spend lots of time loving and gently teaching their babies and toddlers all of the attitudes and ideas they want them to know and to use for a lifetime. If we model kindness and a positive attitude toward life from the time they're born, our children will hopefully carry those lessons with them throughout their lives.

> **L**iving with a toddler is never the same from one day to the next and certainly *never boring*!

This is not to say, however, that we ever stop building that relationship. It is necessary to continue working on it every day in order to keep it healthy.

> **T**he first three years of life are the most important in terms of establishing the bonds of love, trust, and respect for ourselves and others.

A gargantuan amount of patience, understanding, and, above all, good humor are critical ingredients to parenting a toddler! These little ones are on a journey all their own, trying to determine who they are and how they fit into this big world of ours—and they drag us right along with them in the discovery process! We're there to see that they feel good about themselves during this wonderful exploration, to encourage them to try new things when that natural curiosity leads them in new directions, to be there for them whenever they need us, and to create in them a sense of security, trust, and love that they can depend on for the rest of their lives.

Toddlerhood can be a great time for parents, as well, as long as they take rejection with a grain of salt, expect that their lives may be sunny one minute and stormy the next, don't take everything toddlers do or say too seriously (or too personally!), and allow themselves to watch the fascinating process of human discovery with as much awe and excitement as their toddlers do. As long as parents treat their little ones with love and respect, allow them to become the individuals they were meant to be instead of trying to make them into an exact copy of themselves, and help them to approach life positively, their toddlers should develop into pretty competent, self-assured, and loving adults. Try not to worry too much (nobody's perfect and parenting is not a perfect science!), don't let one bad day spoil the next, remember to think positively, and, above all, *enjoy* parenting your toddler! It really is over much too quickly!

ABOUT THE AUTHOR

Judy Schumacher wrote Terrific Toddlers! to encourage empathy and understanding in parents as they learn their way through parenting their toddlers. Parents who role model love, kindness, calm voices and a gentle touch can provide their children with a secure, positive, loving foundation for the rest of their lives.

Judy has been a Family Education Specialist with Saint Paul Public Schools, Senior Program Manager for Success By Six at Twin Cities United Way, and the Director of Education for Minnesota Children's Museum. She holds a Masters degree in Family Education from the University of Minnesota and has had over 25 years of experience in early childhood and parent education.

Judy wishes every parent the very best as they navigate their way through the amazing adventure of raising a toddler!

Made in the USA
Lexington, KY
13 April 2018